# Kawasaki Fours

# Kawasaki Fours

*Mick Walker*

The Crowood Press

## Dedication

To the memory of my son Gary who died competing at Brands Hatch
in September 1994, competing in the sport he loved so much.

First published in 1998 by
The Crowood Press Ltd
Ramsbury, Marlborough
Wiltshire SN8 2HR

**British Library Cataloguing in Publication Data**

A catalogue record for this book is available from the British Library.

ISBN 1 86126 152 7

Frontispiece: The GPZ900R, which set new standards when it appeared in December 1983.

Typeset by Phoenix Typesetting, Ilkley, West Yorkshire.

Printed and bound in Great Britain by The Bath Press.

# Contents

|     | Acknowledgements | 6 |
| 1 | Kawasaki: Engineers to the World | 7 |
| 2 | The Birth of the Kawasaki Motorcycle | 18 |
| 3 | The Z1 | 27 |
| 4 | After Z1 | 41 |
| 5 | The GT Series | 56 |
| 6 | The Z1300 Six | 66 |
| 7 | Turbo | 79 |
| 8 | Touring GTR style | 91 |
| 9 | Custom Cruisers | 98 |
| 10 | The GPZ900R | 106 |
| 11 | Liquid-Cooled Performance | 117 |
| 12 | ZZ-R1100 | 154 |
| 13 | Endurance Racing | 160 |
| 14 | WSB | 171 |
| 15 | Retro | 181 |
|     | Appendix: Kawasaki Owner's Clubs | 189 |
|     | Index | 191 |

# Acknowledgements

The four-cylinder Kawasaki story (I've also included the six-cylinder Z1300 for good measure) is very much one of the modern motorcycle industry, covering as it does the last quarter of a century, beginning with the mould-breaking Z1 of 1972. It is a story dominated by engineering triumphs, but unlike European marques where individuals carve their own legends, the Japanese way is very different, with either committees or a small design team working on a particular project – very rarely will you find an individual taking the credit. The same holds true of the structure, where again it's very much a *team* effort, rather than personal glory.

In the course of compiling this book several people provided information, photographs and personal accounts, and as usual almost to a man (and woman) this was given with a high level of enthusiasm, which is so typical of the motorcycling fraternity. In particular I would like to record my thanks to Peter Richardson and Luke Plummer of the Milton Keynes-based Kawasaki Information Service. Without their help this book would have been much the poorer. Various members of Kawasaki UK, including Simon Belton and Martin Studer, also helped greatly. I also received considerable encouragement for the project from Julie and Jennie Simmonds (wife and daughter) of Kawasaki's first racing champion, the late Dave Simmonds.

Paul Farmer of the British Kawasaki Riders Club was responsible for the club section.

Maurice de Rochefort of Kawasaki Motors France came to the rescue in tracking down some vital material for the Endurance chapter.

Luckily I was able to write this book with the benefit of my personal experiences with several Kawasakis over the years, including a much-loved 1990 model, ZZ-R1100, which had been blueprinted and given a Wiseco big bore kit by its previous owner.

It is now left for me to wish you as much pleasure from reading *Kawasaki Fours* as I have had researching and writing it.

Mick Walker
Wisbech, Cambridgeshire
October 1997

6

# 1 Kawasaki: Engineers to the World

Considering Japan's position as one of the leading industrial nations as we approach the end of the twentieth century, it is hard to appreciate that Japan's own industrial revolution did not occur until the last part of the nineteenth century. Until then, the country was still largely a feudal nation little known to the Western world – indeed, she only opened her ports to foreign traders in 1854, and then only reluctantly. Against such a background, it is clear that when Shozo Kawasaki founded a shipyard at Tsukiji, Tokyo, to construct ocean-going ships in 1878 he was amongst the pioneers of his country's rapid drive towards modernization. Then in 1881, the Kawasaki Hyogo Shipyard was formed at Higashide-cho, Hyogo, and five years on the two yards were combined. A decade later, in 1896, Kawasaki Dockyard was incorporated as a company, with Kojiro Matsukata as its first president; it was re-located at Kobe.

Expansion continued apace, with real diversification beginning in 1906 with establishment of a new factory at Hyogo expressly for the manufacture of railway equipment including locomotives, rolling stock and bridge girders. The next year, production of marine steam turbines began at the dock-yard. During World War I, more muscle was put on with a major new plant to manufacture steel. Then in 1918 the aircraft division was established at the Hyogo Works only fifteen years after the Wright brothers' initial flight, not only to build complete aircraft, but engines too.

During the inter-war years, each division became prominent within its own sphere as a leader in Japanese industry. Dates of importance are: 1919: the marine freight division was split off to form Kawasaki Kisen Kaisha Ltd (K-Line); 1928: the Hyogo Works was split off to become Kawasaki Rolling Stock Manufacturing Co Ltd; 1937: the aircraft division was split off to form Kawasaki Aircraft Co Ltd. It is also important to record that in 1950 the steel-making division was also given its own identity in the shape of Kawasaki Steel Corporation. All these enterprises established a firm foundation in their respective fields both before and after World War II. In the post-war recovery period, aimed at turning Japan into a modern nation, the country soon found itself in an era of rapid economic growth.

In 1969 all Kawasaki's various industrial segments were merged into one giant corporation, Kawasaki Heavy Industries. And it would be true to say that Japan's economic growth is in no small part due to the ships, rolling stock, aircraft, industrial machinery, civil engineering, construction machinery and steel structures built by Kawasaki during this period. The newly created corporation formed the basis for a total engineering organization with deep involvement in myriad projects on land, at sea and in the air.

*Shozo Kawasaki founded a shipyard at Tsukiji, Tokyo to construct ocean-going ships in 1878; almost 120 years later Kawasaki still builds ships – and just about everything else.*

The restructuring merger occurred at a time when there was a growing need for advanced technologies and broad engineering expertise to accomplish many large-scale projects. Ships, rolling stock and aircraft were all becoming bigger, faster and more automated, while land was being developed throughout the nation, and plants were being rebuilt in a drive to drastically improve productivity. Advanced technologies paved the way for the development of outer and inner space, and the world beneath the microscope. Today, however, we are experiencing a backlash in the form of a growing concern to protect the environment and to realize a truly human lifestyle for mankind. Plunged into this new thinking of 'Man and Earth', Kawasaki not only celebrated its 100th anniversary in 1996, but is also set on a new path for the twenty-first century.

Before setting out the layout and aims of Kawasaki Heavy Industries for the present and future, it is important to say that the company has defined six goals for technological development and is conducting the necessary research and development to achieve this. To support these aims Kawasaki has established a three-centre research framework comprising facilities in Akashi (western Japan), Gifu (central Japan) and Kanto (eastern Japan). This framework took shape in February 1995 with the opening of the Kanto Technical Institute, established in the Tokyo area with the objective of further strengthening Kawasaki's exploration of advanced, innovative fields.

As we head for the twenty-first century Kawasaki products can be split into the following groups:

## ROLLING STOCK

This includes the world-famous Shinkansan trains, commuter trains, express trains, locomotives, passenger cars and freight cars. Kawasaki has developed computer-controlled mass-transit systems for

*Expansion continued apace, with real diversification coming in 1906 with the establishment of a new factory at Hyogo expressly for the construction of railway equipment, including locomotives and rolling stock. Ninety years later Kawasaki builds the famous 'Bullet' trains which connect Japanese cities.*

unmanned train operations and automatic train-operating (ATO) devices for one-man train operation; both of these were designed to boost the performance of railroad systems.

Engineering across the whole spectrum of railway traffic systems is another area in which the company excels. Skills include the development and manufacture of wheel lathes, wheel milling machines and other repair systems, audiovisual systems for rolling stock and platform door screen systems.

Kawasaki has a subsidiary in Yonkers, New York, that fabricates and repairs all kinds of passenger and electric cars for the giant American market.

## AIRCRAFT AND JET ENGINES

The aviation industry is considered a knowledge-intensive field, and it is one in which Kawasaki is involved as both a manufacturer of aircraft and engines.

For fixed-wing aircraft, the company supplies portions of the B777 and B767 passenger aircraft developed with the American Boeing Company. Kawasaki also manufacture the T-4 intermediate jet trainer and the P-3C anti-submarine patrol plane. It is also participating in parts production and partial assembly of the F-15 supersonic fighter.

For rotary-wing aircraft, Kawasaki is manufacturing a wide range of helicopters, including the BK117, the helicopter developed in Japan. The company also developed on-board safety systems for helicopters and has successfully conducted a test of the fly-by-wire (FBW) control system on the BK117.

In addition to its involvement in both the manufacture and development of aero engines, the company is participating in the V2500 turbo-fan engine in a joint venture with the UK, the USA, Germany and Italy. Kawasaki is also engaged in basic research programmes for the supersonic transport (SST)/hypersonic transport engines.

## Airpower

The first major contract for the aviation division of what was then the Kawasaki Shipbuilding Company came in 1922 when an order was placed by the Imperial Japanese Army for the construction of 300 licence-built French Salmson 2A2 reconnaissance biplanes. There quickly followed collaboration with Dornier of Germany to build twenty-eight DoN all-metal parasol monoplanes as Army Type 87 heavy bombers. Other Dornier designs built under licence by Kawasaki included Komet four-passenger transports and Merkur six-passenger models. In addition a small number of the well known Wal all-metal commercial flying boats were also constructed under licence.

*Kawasaki's Ki10, the Japanese army's last biplane fighter. It served during the Chinese conflict, prior to World War II.*

*Designed by Takeo Doi and Shin Owada, the Kawasaki Ki61 Hein (Swallow) was the first Japanese fighter monoplane with a liquid-cooled engine (a licence-built German Daimler Benz) The year was 1941.*

Dipl. Ing. Richard Vogt was appointed as chief designer in the late 1920s, and he was the man who was largely responsible for converting the Japanese company from foreign licence-built models to Japanese-conceived aircraft. Some of his best designs included the Type 88 reconnaissance, the Type 92 fighter and the Type 93 light bomber. Vogt returned to Germany in the mid-1930s to take up a post with Blohm und Voss, and his successor was Takeo Doi, who with the assistance of engineers Imachi and Tojo designed the successful Ki10, the last of the Japanese Army's biplane fighters. Then came the Ki32 light bomber, the Ki45 heavy fighter, the Ki48 medium bomber and Kawasaki's most famous fighter of the war, the Ki61 Hein (Swallow).

With its liquid-cooled engine (a licence-built German Daimler Benz DB601), long tapered nose and wings of high aspect ratio, the Ki61 was unique among Nipponese fighter aircraft of World War II and it marked the first attempt by the Japanese Army Air Force to incorporate in a fighter design the armour protection and self-sealing fuel tank which had been shown to be indispensible by early war reports received from Europe.

One of the most impressive post-war Kawasaki aircraft has been the C-1A military transport for the Japanese Air Self-Defence Force. The first prototype took to the air in November 1970 and was followed into service by the production model. A high-wing monoplane with swept-back wings, it was powered by a pair of Pratt & Whitney turbo fan engines and could carry sixty fully equipped troops; its maximum speed was 506mph (814km/h). Another successful Kawasaki design has been the T4 Blue Impulse advanced jet trainer.

There have also been a number of American aircraft built by Kawasaki under licence, including the Lockhead P-3C anti-submarine patrol plane, the T-33 jet trainer and the Boeing CH-47 twin-engined helicopter.

*Today, the Kawasaki aircraft division builds both fixed wing and helicopter types.*

## SPACE DEVELOPMENT EQUIPMENT

The technology that Kawasaki has acquired from the development and manufacture of aircraft is now being applied to space. A geodetic satellite developed and assembled by Kawasaki was launched by the H-I rocket in 1986. Today the satellite continues to send vital information from its orbit, 995 miles (1,600km) above the earth.

Kawasaki, having overseen the construction of the H-II rocket launch complex, has also been in charge of its payload fairing project. The company is, moreover, engaged in other space projects that include the H-II orbiting plane 'HOPE', the Japanese Experiment Module (JEM) – part of the Space Station Programme – and rendezvous and docking systems. In addition, Kawasaki is involved with astronaut training.

## ENVIRONMENTAL PROTECTION

Like many other large industrial complexes, Kawasaki is making an effort to develop technologies to help protect the environment. The company has developed flue gas desulphurization and denitrification systems, steel converter exhaust gas treatment systems and other anti-pollution systems for power plants, steel and cement plants and facilities.

Kawasaki is making similar efforts in the field of waste and sewage treatment, the need for which is becoming ever more important as the quality of living improves and industrial progress advances.

## RESOURCES RECYLING

Kawasaki has developed a wide range of systems, many of which are already in operation, to recover useful resources from industrial and household refuse, including waste materials from building and road construction sites, old furniture and office equipment. The soil recycling system, for example, crushes waste from road construction and then mixes it with improving agents. The resulting material can be used as filling material.

## ENERGY PLANTS

Currently Kawasaki is directing major efforts toward this sector, with the development of gas turbines in particular. This is because of their outstanding performance and efficiency, the latter offering a potentially effective solution to environmental problems. The company is also carrying out long-term R & D projects in the field of atomic energy, including development of fast breeder reactors (FBRs) and hot gas furnaces, as well as fusion reactors.

## CIVIL ENGINEERING AND CONSTRUCTION MACHINERY

Civil engineering and construction projects grow ever larger in scale. Consequently, the machines used in these projects need to have increasingly large capacities and ever greater levels of efficiency. They also have to be completely safe to operate and contribute to the working environment. An entire project has to be engineered as a complete package.

The range of machinery produced by Kawasaki is vast, including machines for excavation (earth-moving and material-handling) and ground preparation. The company's machines include the huge tunnel-boring equipment used in the construction of the Eurotunnel under the

*Kawasaki supplied the huge tunnel-boring equipment used by the French in the construction of the Eurotunnel under the Straits of Dover.*

Straits of Dover, the world's largest shield machines with a diameter of 14.14m (46.3ft), wheel loaders and large belt conveyors, and a wide variety of road-compacting and concrete-paving equipment.

## STEEL STRUCTURES

Advanced-quality steel structure technology is vital in national land development and in the consolidation of the industrial infra-structure – in, for example, high-rise buildings, long-span bridges and large-scale industrial and power generation complexes.

Kawasaki designs and fabricates steel structures of almost limitless diversity. Recently the company was responsible for a main tower of the Akashi Kaikyo Bridge – when finished, this bridge will be the longest suspension type in the world. Its expertise also includes construction of airport hangars, rocket launching complexes and other large-scale high-profile structures.

## PLANT ENGINEERING

Kawasaki is one of the world's foremost engineering experts for all kinds of plants, ranging from steel, cement and chemical through to food processing, prefabricated housing and other consumer-oriented types. The company not only plans, designs, builds and tests such plants; it also develops and manufactures the main equipment used in them.

## AUTOMATION, LABOUR-SAVING AND DISTRIBUTION SYSTEMS

Automation has brought, and will bring, ever increasing efficiency improvements in manufacturing, processing and logistics systems. Kawasaki is a market leader in a wide range of industrial robots for assembling, handling, welding, painting, sealing and virtually every other need.

Kawasaki has also created water-jet cuffing systems and $CO_2$ laser systems, as well as the world's first using an iodine laser.

*Automation is another area in which Kawasaki is a market leader, with a wide range of industrial robots for assembly, handling, welding, painting, sealing and just about any other requirement.*

## JET SKI®, ALL-TERRAIN VECHICLES, GENERAL PURPOSE ENGINES AND MOTORCYCLES

Jet Ski®, all-terrain vehicles (ATV), portable generators and motorcycles are just some of the Kawasaki consumer products that have made the brand name a household word around the world. In 1950 Kawasaki designed and built its first motorcycle engine, a 148cc four-stroke. More followed, and in 1953 a company was set up to exclusively distribute these engines which were fitted into other manufacturers' machines. The first all-Kawasaki motorcycle was the BI, a 125cc two-stroke of 1962. It was also Kawasaki's first consumer product. Today Kawasaki's range stretches from utilitarian 50cc bikes to a thundering 1,500cc V-twin cruiser, and is headed by the flagship ZZ-R1100 four-cylinder sports tourer.

The Jet Ski® personal watercraft were first produced in Kawasaki's American Lincoln facilities more than two decades ago, and started a whole new craze in marine sports. Jet Skis® can now be found on beaches and lakes right around the globe.

With thirteen plants worldwide, including the Akashi works in Japan, the home of the Consumer Products Group, Kawasaki offers a truly diverse range of consumer products which also include multipurpose, four-wheel vehicles (originally also with three-wheel construction, a switch was made to four wheels on safety grounds a decade ago) and portable generators ranging from 500 to 5,000 watts.

Finally, with its range of small general-purpose engines (ranging from 0.6hp to 20hp), Kawasaki products are also a leading power source for agricultural, industrial, civil engineering and construction applications.

*The Jet Ski personal watercraft, which were first produced in Kawasaki's American Lincoln plant more than two decades ago, started a whole new craze in marine sports.*

*One of thirteen plants worldwide, the Akashi works in Japan is the home of Kawasaki's Consumer Product Group and manufactures all-terrain vehicles, small general-purpose engines, Jet Skis and, most importantly as far as this book is concerned, motorcycles.*

But of all Kawasaki's vast range of products and services, there is no doubt that its motorcycles display the secret of its success, that of offering balanced performance, high quality, reliability and modern styling all in a single package. And in its four-cylinder designs more than any other, this genius has been realized to the full.

Read on and discover just what has been achieved in the last quarter of a century since the birth of the mould-breaking Z1 which burst onto the scene at the Cologne Show in September 1972.

---

## Factories and Main Products

| *Factories* | *Products* |
|---|---|

**Noda Works** — **Steel structures:** steel frames; airport facilities and equipment; steel pipe structures; steel towers; bridges; steel hydraulic pipes; steel water pipes; flood gates; LNG tanks; LPG tanks; other tanks; high-pressure gas containers; steel stacks; blast furnaces; alloy hydrogen storage equipment

**Yachiyo Works** — **Recycling equipment for plants and resources:** iron ore crushers and graders; material coal crushers; COM manufacturing facilities; bulky refuse and iron scrap crushers; excavated soil-recycling facilities; slag-recycling facilities; aggregate manufacturing facilities; pulverizing mill; various breakers, crushers and driers.
**Crushers, breakers, sieves and driers:** gyratory crushers; jaw crushers; impeller crushers; vertical mills; rod mills; ball mills; shredders; feeders; vibratory sieves; pulverizers; dredge pumps
**Moulding steel and cast-iron products:** wear-resistant special cast-iron products; heat-and-wear-resistant special cast-iron products; precision machined cast-iron products

**Chiba Works** — **Plants:** thermal power generation plant; oxygen converter gas-treating equipment; municipal refuse incinerators; ash-sluicing equipment
**Boilers:** Benson boilers; industrial boilers; recycling boilers; special fuel boilers; various waste heat boilers; maritime application boilers
**Others:** air-cooled heat exchangers; nuclear machinery

**Sodegaura Works** — **Steel structures:** bridges; various tanks; conventional steel products

**Gifu Works** — **Airplanes:** manufacturing, repair and overhaul of equipment relating to commercial airplanes; antisubmarine airplanes; fighters; trainers; helicopters; missiles and space equipment

**Nagoya Works 1** — **Airplanes:** manufacturing and assembly of structural airplane parts

**Nagoya Works 2** — **Airplanes:** manufacturing and assembly of structural airplane parts

**Kobe Works** — **Ships and maritime application equipment:** ultra high-speed passenger ships (Jetfoil); high-speed car ferries (Jet Piercer); submarines; various types of ship; research ships; repair and modification of ships
**Engines:** steam turbines for ground and maritime applications; gas turbines for ground and maritime applications; diesel engines for ground and maritime applications; large accelerators and decelerators; propellers; water-jet propulsors; air blowers; air compressors; natural gas force-feeding modules; wind tunnels; tunnel ventilation systems
**Factory automation devices:** water-jet cutting system (KAWACA); $CO_2$ laser system; steel structure CAD/CAM system (ADEL); shaped steel fabrication system (COM); vibrating machines; physical distribution systems

| | |
|---|---|
| Hyogo Works | **Trains**: electric locomotives; electric cars; passenger coaches; railcars; fuelled railcars; new traffic systems; freight cars; tank cars<br>**Others**: high pressure vessels; straddle cranes (K lift); aerial ropeways; cable cars; monorail cars; platform doors |
| Nishi-Kobe Works | **Hydraulic equipment**: pumps; motors; valves; rotary actuators; hydraulic units; hydraulic systems for industrial use<br>**Maritime application machines**: electric hydraulic steering devices; automatic steering machines; deck machinery; deck cranes; fishing machinery<br>**Others**: precision gear pumps for chemical fibre spinning; test and simulation equipment; manipulators; brushless servomotors |
| Seishin Works | **Jet engines**: jet engines; parts of gas turbines |
| Akashi Works | **Motorcycles, engines** etc: motorcycles; all-terrain vehicles (ATVs); Jet Ski personal watercraft; engines; engine-powered electric generators; transmissions<br>**Jet engines**: manufacturing and overhaul of jet engines and gas turbines; transmissions for helicopters<br>**Industrial gas turbines, powered equipment**: gas turbine generator sets; gas turbine cogeneration systems; mechanical drive gas turbine sets; mobil gas turbine generator sets<br>**Robots**: spot-welding robots; arc-welding robots; coating and sealing robots; handling robots; assembly robots; muscular function evaluation and training machines |
| Banshu Works | **Construction machinery and cargo-handling equipment**: wheel loaders; tire rollers; macadam rollers; vibratory rollers; mine application load carriers; rotary drills; snow ploughs; concrete paving machines; concrete mixers; log loaders; fork loaders; towing tractors; load haul-dumps |
| Harima Works | **Plants and antipollution machinery**; steel-making plants; cement plants; petrochemical plants; coal and chemical plants; chemical fibre plants; sugar plants; fertilizer plants; cross-current centrifugal extractors; heat exchangers; dust collectors; water-processing facilities; waste gas desulphicrization/denitrification plants<br>**Construction machinery**: shield boring machines; tunnel excavators; vertical excavators; belt conveyors; bucket wheel excavators<br>**Steel construction**: steel frames; airport facilities and equipment; steel pipe structures; bridges; LNG tanks; LPG tanks; other tanks; high-pressure gas vessels; subterranean tunnels; maritime structures; steel hydraulic pipes; water gates; steel stacks; launchers; container-handling cranes; ramp ways |
| Sakaide Works | **Ships and maritime application equipment**: tankers; bulk carriers; LNG carriers; LPG carriers; container ships; car carriers; oil-drilling rigs; self-elevated maritime operation platforms; floating docks; various plant barges; repair and modification of ships |

# 2 The Birth of the Kawasaki Motorcycle

When World War II ended, Kawasaki, unlike the majority of other Japanese companies, found its engineering skill in such demand that only one of its many plants was standing idle. But eventually this too found a market niche to keep it busy, providing engine and gearbox assemblies for the rapidly emerging motorcycle industry. It was in 1950, just as the Korean War was about to get under way, that Kawasaki engineers designed and built their first-ever motorcycle engine. This was a 148cc ohv four-stroke (model KE) with a single vertical cylinder and four-speed gearbox; it was used by Fuji, Gasuden and IMC amongst others. Development of other engines of different capacities continued apace until 1953, when a separate company was created, exclusively to market and distribute these engines to a by now relatively large number of motorcycle builders.

*The assembly plant in Kobe, producing Meihatsu motorcycles during the 1950s; engine assemblies were of Kawasaki manufacture.*

One of Kawasaki's major customers was the old-established Maguro concern, and it was with this marque that Kawasaki took its first hesitant steps towards becoming a motorcycle manufacturer in its own right. The move could be traced back to 1959 when a motorcycle research and development centre was instigated. From this came a new assembly plant in Akashi which was completed in 1960, and late the same year Maguro became affiliated to Kawasaki Aircraft. This bond was strengthened in 1961 when there was a further move to join Kawasaki and Maguro into one corporate identity, with its financial headquarters in Tokyo. In mid-1961, Kawasaki Auto Sales was created; and then in 1962 came the first model to carry a Kawasaki badge, the 124cc (54 x 54mm) B8, a single-cylinder two-stroke. It produced 8bhp at 6,000rpm; other features included a unit construction four-speed gearbox, 16in wheels, drum brakes, telescopic forks and swinging arm rear suspension – in reality hardly anything to set it out from the norm of Japanese lightweight commuter bikes. Except, of course, that unlike the opposition it was backed by a major international industrial player.

It was probably this latter point which saw the B8 being exported, albeit in modest numbers, to the USA in 1964, where the company set up a branch office in Los Angeles. The main purpose of this move was not simply to follow the likes of Honda, Suzuki and Yamaha who were already selling bikes in the States, but to research the market in that vast country. A year later Kawasaki opened another branch office, this time on the eastern seaboard, with Chicago chosen as the location. Incidentally the 125 was marketed in the USA under the Omega brand, but with very little success, it has to be said. But what was of vital importance was the market research, which was to prove of great help over the next few years. Essentially this told Kawasaki that machines developed for utility use in Japan had limited potential in the American

*The first Kawasaki-badged motorcycle, the 125cc B8 single cylinder two-stroke, circa 1962.*

## Dave Simmonds:
## Kawasaki's First World Champion

Although Kawasaki raced their four-cylinder 125 two-stroke in domestic events and the Singapore Grand Prix, it was never destined to reach Europe. Instead, the company's English rider, Dave Simmonds, was provided with an updated twin for 1967; but this was to prove an uphill struggle on the GP scene that year for both rider and manufacturer. In addition, Dave suffered a serious crash at the Ulster round (whilst riding a 250) which was to sideline him for almost all the following year.

Into 1969 and the Englishman still had the loan of his by now ageing works 125. With Yamaha officially quitting the sport, Simmonds secretly thought that he just might at last stand a chance of that elusive grand prix victory. However, in case the term 'works rider' conjures up the image of a group of factory mechanics in beautifully laundered overalls and a motorhome, just ponder this: Dave Simmonds was very much on his own, one man riding and working on his Kawasaki, his base a caravan-cum-workshop lit by bottled gas.

*Kawasaki's first world champion. Against all the odds, Englishman Dave Simmonds became Kawasaki first-ever world champion in 1969.*

If the truth be known, prior to the start of the 1969 season, the factory had privately given up all hope of not only winning a world championship, but also of even securing a single GP victory. In fact, just before the season got underway, as Dave remarked afterwards: 'They sent me a box containing two crankshafts, four pistons, a few sets of piston rings and various smaller components such as gaskets and oil seals. It was virtually all they had left in stock. That was it, and the best of luck!' With this in mind, what actually transpired is all the more amazing: over an eleven-round championship, Dave won no less than eight rounds, and this after missing the first in Spain because he didn't have the start money!

However, if the above paints a picture of a faultless mechanical tune, nothing could be further from the truth. Almost from the start, Dave suffered endless problems during practice, and qualified with the barest minimum of laps; but then he had a virtually trouble-free race after never really getting a flying start.

Dave Simmonds tragically met his death, not on the race circuit, but in heroically trying to put out a fire in another competitor's caravan at Rungis, a suburb of Paris, in 1972. He is survived today by his wife Julie and daughter Jennie.

*Simmonds' championship-winning 125 Kawasaki disc valve twin.*

market – as had been proven by the B8's relative lack of sales. Kawasaki also realized from an early stage that it was vitally important to hire American staff, listen to them and then build what the locals wanted to buy. And this they did, with great success. The B8 ran till 1966, and by then the pot was just beginning to boil with a whole host of new motorcycle designs under development.

The first real attempt by Kawasaki to enter the big bike league had come the previous year with the arrival of the 624cc (74 x 72.66mm) WI. This was very much an inherited Maguro, itself a close copy of the British BSA pre-unit A7/10 twin-cylinder models. The 360-degree parallel twin had pushrod-operated valves and it produced a claimed 50bhp at 6,500 rpm. Other variants

of the basic theme were the WISS (1968–71), the W2SS Commander (1968–70) and the street scrambler W2TT Commander (1969). But of course it wasn't to be a rehash of what was largely an outmoded design which really began Kawasaki's drive to the top; instead it was a series of ultra-modern, high performance two-strokes, in both twin- and three-cylinder guises.

The first model was the AI Samurai twin, which made its public bow in May 1966. The 247cc (53 x 56mm) engine was unusual for a streetbike in that it featured disc-valve induction and thus side-mounted carburettors with the attendant problems of width, inlet trunking and primary drive. Kawasaki's development team set to offset this by mounting the generator behind the

*Derived from the earlier Maguro design (itself based on the BSA A7/10 series), the Kawasaki 650 WISS was built from 1968 through to 1971.*

*Kawasaki's A1 Samurai 247cc disc valve twin. There was also the larger 338cc A7 Avenger. The Samurai first appeared in 1966.*

cylinders rather than on the crankshaft end. The Samurai and its larger 338cc A7 Avenger brother were the first Kawasaki motorcycles to sell well in the important American market. There were also a pair of customer racing versions – Kawasaki's first 'over-the-counter' twin-cylinder to be offered for sale in the shape of the A1R (250) and A7R (350) machines.

However, the models which really put Kawasaki on the international map in the early days were a series of three-cylinder, piston-port two-strokes. The first of these, the fearsome H1 (Mach III), appeared in time for the 1969 season. Its 498.8cc (60 x 58.8mm) engine produced 60bhp at

7,500rpm, this being progressively detuned over the following years until by 1976 it was down to only 52bhp. But make no mistake, for its era that original H1 was a real flyer, capable of approaching 120mph (190km/h) with ease; the proviso being that its rider had the nerve to keep the throttle pinned, as handling certainly wasn't its forte. Along the way the H1 became the H1A (1971), H1B (1972), H1D (1973), H1E (1974), H1F (1975) and finally the KH500 in 1976.

If the H1 could be described as exciting, then the H2 (Mach IV) was truly awesome. This followed the same basic two-stroke, three-cylinder engine formula, but with the capacity increased to 748cc (71 x 63mm).

*But it was the three-cylinder two-stroke 500 H1 (Mach 111) of 1969 which really put Kawasaki into the motorcycling spotlight. For its time it was a real flyer (120mph / 193km/h), although handling left much to be desired.*

*Three-cylinder Kawasaki engine production line, 1970.*

*Tom Pemberton taking victory on a 500 Mach 111 at Snetterton in the early 1970s – note those bell-bottoms!*

With maximum power of 74bhp at 6,800rpm, performance, at least in a straight line, was the equal of any production streetbike of its era. Unfortunately the Mach IV's 130mph (210km/h) maximum speed and arm-wrenching acceleration were rather blunted by a jaw-dropping low of 12mpg (24l/100km) when this performance was exploited to the full! The 750 Mach IV ran from 1971 through to 1975. Like the 250 and 350 disc-valve twins, there were racing versions of the Mach III and Mach IV, in the shape of the H1R and H2R respectively. Other Kawasaki triples included the S1 (249.5cc),

S2 (346cc) and S3 (399cc); the S1 became the KH250 in 1976, the S3 the KH400 in the same year.

The world oil crisis of 1974 was what really killed off the high performance two-strokes from 'Big K', the company being forced to explore the four-stroke path in its quest to establish itself as Japan's premier performance motorcycle builder. But as described in subsequent chapters, Kawasaki was already well on the way to 'alternative' power with the launch in September 1972 of its four-cylinder double overhead cam Z1 Superbike.

*Mick Grant cresting the 'Mountain' at Cadwell Park in 1977 aboard one of the fearsome factory 750 three-cylinder racers.*

*Built in 250 and 350 forms, the inline (tandem) disc valve twins gained Kawasaki no less than eight road racing world titles between 1978 and 1982.*

*Close-up of the prototype (motocross) Uni-Trak system, 1979.*

*Four-times world champion Kork Ballington pictured here with his team in 1981. The bike is the KR500 monoque-framed, four-cylinder two-stroke. His titles were gained with the smaller 250/350 twins.*

*French-Canadian Yvon du Hamel made a big name for himself and Kawasaki during the period 1971–77.*

*German Anton Mang, double world champion (250 and 350cc) for Kawasaki in 1981.*

*Watercooling was first used by Kawasaki on its motocross (shown) and racing bikes. This picture dates from June 1980 and shows a factory prototype KX125W.*

*Brad Lackey's factory Kawasaki motocross GP bike, July 1979. It was the first to use the Uni-Trak monoshock rear suspension system.*

# 3　The Z1

One motorcycle more than any other established the Japanese industry as constructors of large capacity, high performance muscle bikes: that machine was Kawasaki's Z1. Although the first the public saw of the Z1 was in September 1972 at the Cologne Show, work on the project had begun back in 1967 – before the Mach III two-stroke triple had even hit the market! Originally known under the code NYS (New York Streak), the aim was to provide Kawasaki with a big-bore four-stroke replacement for the then current W-series parallel twin. They carried out extensive research, which revealed a need for a sports tourer with a surplus of power,

capable of hauling two people and full equipment over both short and long distances. It also needed to meet current and predicted future emission standards, as the vast bulk of the projected sales figures would come from the giant American market.

To achieve the targets set from the above priorities it soon became evident that the new design needed to be a four-stroke of at least 750cc and equipped with double overhead camshafts. Finally, to provide the required sophistication it would need at least four cylinders. During 1968 design began in earnest and clay mock-ups were built. Engineering and styling teams worked their

*Originally Kawasaki intended a '750' – until rivals Honda came up with their CB750. Then the project was upped to a 900. The result was the Z1. One of the initial production batch is seen here, on 20 September 1972.*

way through a whole series of problems which could have potentially swamped a less able group of engineers.

Meanwhile Kawasaki management were confidently looking forward to the next few years with growing enthusiasm, believing as they did that their new four would run in tandem alongside the yet-to-be-released H1 triple. The latter certainly made an impact when it was launched in September 1968, and its combination of a fiery 498.8cc, 60bhp three-cylinder two-stroke engine and relatively light weight ensured exhilarating performance. But it took a brave man to extract the best from it due to less-than-perfect handling qualities, whilst its thirst was always an embarrassment.

The other problem for Kawasaki was Honda, or to be more precise one machine: the CB750, which stunned the motorcycling fraternity when it was launched at the Tokyo Show in October 1968. The CB750 was not of course the first four, and as we prove here, it was certainly nothing new. But the Honda was still one of the most influential motorcycles of all time, certainly on a par with Edward Turner's Triumph Speed Twin of the late 1930s, for the trend it set for standard

---

## Early Fours

Unlike elsewhere in Europe, Victorian England was still very much a society dominated by horse-power. There was a vast array of draconian regulations impeding the development of self-propelled vehicles, including a speed limit of 4mph (6km/h). It was only in 1896 with the passing of the Emancipation Act, that these restrictions were lifted and the new transport industries began to flourish. Despite this, it was an Englishman, Major (later Colonel) Henry Capel Lofft Holden, who built the world's first four-cylinder motorcycle in 1897.

Variable gears were still well over a decade ahead, so Holden relied instead on sheer power to overcome the inherent inflexibility of direct drive. Like the German pioneers, Hildebrand & Wolfmüller, he employed long, exposed connecting rods and cranks linked directly to the rear wheel spindle; however his engine differed greatly from the Munich product.

The four cylinders were placed in horizontal pairs, each like a straight unpinned pipe, closed at both ends. In each pipe was a long piston with a crown at each end, and explosions took place at alternate ends of the cylinders, giving an impulse on each stroke. With a total capacity of 1,047cc (54 x 114mm), substantial gudgeon pins or 'crosshead' pins as used on a steam railway engine, projected through slots in the cylinder walls to engage with the connecting rods. Automatic inlet valves were employed, but the mechanically operated exhaust valves, lacking any convenient rotary motion in the engine to drive them, were actuated via a camshaft, chain-driven from the machine's rear wheel.

The four-cylinder Holden engine operated at a mere 420rpm, at which it produced 3bhp which gave a maximum speed of 24mph (39km/h). Limited production was undertaken by the Kennington, London-based concern, but a change to water cooling was needed as early prototypes suffered over-heating glitches. Originally production had been planned to start in 1898, but it was not until the following year, 1899, that it actually got under way. Unfortunately watercooling added to the already considerable weight of the Holden four, so it fared badly against the smaller cars which offered superior comfort, reliability and price. However, three examples were exhibited at the 1901 Stanley Show, and one was ridden from London to Petersfield and back, some 106 miles (170km), without trouble; but that marked the swansong of the world's first 'Superbike'. An 1897 prototype of the Holden survives today in London's Science Museum.

Other early four-cylinder motorcycles included the Belgian FN, Austro-Hungarian Laurin & Klement, and the German Dürkopp.

production machines. Besides the specification which included a 736.5cc (61 x 63mm) four cylinder with sohc, five-speed gearbox, electric starter, disc front brake and a four-pipe exhaust, Honda's other ace was price. All earlier attempts to market multi-cylinder machines had been limited to small-scale production because of high prices. Quite simply Honda made its model *affordable*.

The CB750 considerably influenced the design of what was to emerge as the Z1, Kawasaki being forced to go further than it might otherwise have done in size and specification. Although Kawasaki had been deeply shocked by the emergence of the Honda, it was soon realized that it was a positive, rather than negative happening. For one thing it allowed the company to see what the market reaction was to a large capacity, across-the-frame four, it enabled it to study the opposition's design in detail, to read what the press thought, and even to strip one down to the last nut and bolt! By the end of 1969 the original NYS project was given an upgrade – an increase to 900cc and more power than originally envisaged. Early the following year development went into overdrive, and by mid-1970 the project team was centralized with styling, engine and chassis groups all working as one team.

By Christmas the prototype of the new machine was well advanced and in the spring of 1971 it was wheeled out on the Yatabe test circuit. But although an impressive-looking bike, and with 95bhp and a 140mph-plus (225km/h) maximum speed, there were problems, mainly associated with deforming of pistons, lubrication and the breather system. However, the engineers worked their way through the difficulties, and as they did everyone began to realize that here was a design with real potential. With the United States of America as its major market, the next phase was to ship two prototypes to Los Angeles as part of the ongoing test programme. These were then subjected to both short journey city use and long distance, including Los Angeles to Daytona and back. These two machines were also given a thorough workout on various race circuits.

*The British launch of the Z1 came at London's Earl's Court Show in November 1972. British importers at the time were Agrati Sales of Nottingham.*

The only real problem was that final drive chains wore out at an alarming rate; then it was back to Japan to be examined in detail.

After this they were reassembled and returned once more to the USA for the final portion of the test programme. Finally, in June 1972, many of the world's motorcycle journalists were invited to Japan to view the definitive machine and their opinions and criticisms requested. Production had already begun a month earlier, but at a slow rate – simply to meet the needs of the forthcoming launch. This took place in Germany at the Cologne Show in September 1972, and was followed up by exhibitions at Paris and Oslo, and also in London, where at Earl's Court British Kawasaki importers, Agrati Sales of Nottingham, gave the Z1 its UK debut.

Any worries that Kawasaki might have harboured were instantly quelled by a flood of orders from not just its natural market in north America, but from all around the world. Official factory records show that by 1975 production was running at some 5,000 units per month. This was helped by the completion of a four-stroke-only assembly facility which had opened in late summer 1972. But what made the Z1 such a success was its real 'Superbike' image, based around a clever mix of advanced engineering and practical rider-friendly features. For example, even though it was equipped with double overhead camshafts, the Z1 engine was relatively simple to service. With the engine still installed in the chassis, the cylinder head and block could be removed, as could such components as the gearchange mechanism, clutch and starter. Only if the crankshaft or gearbox needed attention was a major stripdown called for.

*The Z1's 903cc (66 x 66mm) air-cooled dohc engine cut away to expose its innermost working features*

*The Japanese-only Z2; compared with the Z1's 82bhp, the Z2's 69bhp meant that as both bikes weighed the same, performance was far less impressive.*

Actually the big Z (or 'Zee', as the Americans called it) was built in two engine sizes: the conventional Z1 – 903cc (66 x 66mm), or the Japanese Z2 – only 746cc (64 x 58mm), the larger 'export' model giving 82bhp at 8,500rpm, and the home market model 69bhp at 9,000rpm. As both bikes weighed in at 230kg (507lb), the Z1 had much the superior performance, both from top speed and torque figures. Although both Zs were modern in appearance and specification, it was their engines which commanded the lion's share of attention. As if to confound reason they were not only capable of breathtaking performance, but were also quiet, docile and able to run on regular grade fuel.

The assembly was cast in the classic mould of the across-the-frame four layout already used on factory racing machines such as MV Agusta, Gilera, Benelli and of course Honda, the outer pistons moving together in opposition to the central pair. As was normal Japanese practice, the crankcase split horizontally on the crankshaft and contained the gearbox. The crankshaft was an all-caged roller affair with no less than six main bearings supporting it, with the central pair clamped to the upper crankcase half. The crank was pressed together with the main-shafts forged with the webs, and these shaped to provide the balance factor. With a built-up crankshaft, one-piece rods could be employed. The three-ring pistons ran a compression ratio of 8.5:1; an alloy cylinder carried pressed-in iron liners. The cylinder block featured a tunnel cast into its centre from the cam drive chain.

The valve seats were cast in the head and manufactured in an extra-hard material enabling the engine to run on lead-free fuel. The valves themselves operated in bronze guides, and this material proved to be one of the few errors the design team made. Its wear rate was too fast for comfort, and in later years it was substituted for iron, this becoming a retro-fit replacement for all Z1 (and Z2) motors. Each valve used duplex coil springs, and valve adjustment was by the shim-set method. Both camshafts ran in four pairs of split plain bearings. The exhaust camshaft featured an integral skew gear to drive the tacho.

The lubrication system was of the wet sump variety and took care of not just the engine, but the gearbox and primary drive. The main oil feed was connected to a pressure switch mounted in the upper section of the crankcase next to the engine breather. This was part of what Kawasaki termed 'positive crankcase ventilation' (PCV), which was already widely used in car engines to reduce emissions.

Carburation was taken care of by a quartet of Mikuni VM28 instruments with round slides and separate starter circuits; these were all mounted on a single plate enabling them to be removed as a complete assembly. Ignition was by conventional coil and battery, with two sets of points under the offside crankshaft end cover. The Z1 employed an electric starter (there was also a back-up kickstart) and a twelve-volt system. An interesting feature of the Z1/2 was the second oil pump; this was driven by the gearbox output shaft and supplied oil to the final drive chain. There was a small tank under the seat and lubricant reached

its target via a non-return valve which passed it into the gearbox shaft. From there it was 'thrown' out through holes onto the chain as the shaft rotated. The transmission of the Z1/2 was extremely simple, and sensibly provided with the very minimum number of components, thus cutting down on what could potentially go wrong. Primary transmission was a spur gear set, this being manufactured in the easiest, most cost-effective way. At the front the gear was cut on the metal of the inner web of the most offside cylinder, and so was an inherent section of the crankshaft. Behind, the second gear ran on a needle race mounted on the gearbox input shaft and drove the clutch drum via shock-absorbing springs.

The clutch was wet multi-plate with eight friction and seven plain discs all clamped by five springs.

The gearbox was all indirect with five speeds and crossover drive. Ball races supported the shafts behind the clutch and final drive sprocket, with needle bearings at the other ends.

Other details included a duplex cradle

---

## Kawasaki's First Four

Kawasaki's first four-cylinder motorcycle was not, as everyone imagines, the new legendary Z1 Superbike, but a little-known racing prototype of the mid-1960s. At the 1966 Japanese road race grand prix at the Fisco circuit, Kawasaki not only entered 90 and 250cc models in the Junior clubman-type events, but both twin *and* four-cylinder bikes in the 125GP event. The existence of the latter was at the time completely unknown to the press and public alike, until the tiny four was wheeled out for the first qualifying session.

Naomi Tanaguchi, a former Honda works rider and development tester, had joined the Kawasaki race department. And it was Tanaguchi who rode the four, the twins being piloted by the former MZ and Suzuki star Ernst Degner, the British duo of Dave Simmonds and Chris Vincent, plus local rider Araoka. Although the four was never raced in a classic counting towards the world championships again, it did race abroad, notably in the Singapore GP in 1967, where Araoka and Tanaguchi finished third and fourth respectively.

Probably because of the FIM's twin cylinder ruling which was introduced for the 1969 season, development of the interesting liquid-cooled, disc valve, four-carb model was abandoned in favour of the 125 twin, on which Dave Simmonds later took the 1969 world title.

frame, exposed stanchion telescopic front forks, and three-position adjustable rear shocks. Both wheels were built up with wire spokes and chrome-plated steel rims, with the front fitted with a 3.25 x 19 tyre and the rear a 4.00 x 18. The hydraulically operated front brake featured a single working piston caliper and 296mm stainless steel disc. And there is no doubt that Kawasaki (and the rest of the Japanese industry) needed several tries at providing a suitable disc and pad material combination.

At the rear, a 200mm single leading shoe drum brake tried its best to cope with the undoubted speed potential of the Z1. For anyone comparing one of these machines with any of the current range of Japanese retro models there is a major shortfall in braking performance. This is far more noticeable than the power or handling of the respective machines.

Generally the Z1 received rave reviews from the world's motorcycling press, except in Britain where the importers Agrati only brought in some ten to twelve machines. Speaking to Arthur Bullock (longtime Agrati technical manager) recently, he says that Kawasaki upped prices to such a degree that it became impossible to continue as the importer. In any case, Agrati relinquished the Kawasaki concession and became Benelli importers in October 1973. As is described elsewhere in this book, Kawasaki themselves then took on the responsibility of distribution in the UK. The result was a dearth of Z1s sold in Britain during 1973.

For 1974 the Z1 became the Z1A. Changes were minimal: the black finish on the head, cylinder and crankcases was dropped in favour of a natural alloy finish, a stop-light warning bulb was added, there was improvement to carburation and ignition, plus new colours and graphics – and that was all.

*The late Dick Emery, TV comedian and life-long keen motorcyclist; seen here with his chosen mount in 1974, a Z1A.*

1975 brought the Z1B and more changes, including a sealed rear chain and the removal of the chain oil pump and its tank. Internally a new two-piece head gasket was adopted, whilst the primary drive was modified to cut down on gear whine (the latter measure was introduced mid-year). There were again new colours.

A year on and the 1976 mould was coded Z900-A4. This saw a reduction in carb size – down from 28 to 26mm – but other refinements meant that overall power was not affected to any real degree. More noticeable were twin discs at the front and these were lighter in an attempt to reduce unsprung weight. Again there were new colours, and also a locking filler cap which used the same key as the ignition and seat lock.

## Daytona Record-Breaking Efforts

March 1973 saw the Z1 take part in a series of record attempts at Daytona. Riding a specially tuned 124bhp Yoshimura-prepared Z1, French-Canadian racing star Yvon du Hamel set a new lap record for the Daytona tri-oval at a searing 169.19mph (272.23km/h). Du Hamel also broke the Moto Guzzi-held world records for the 10 and 100 kilometres (6 and 60 miles) with speeds of 150.84mph (242.70km/h) and 141.82mph (228.19km/h) respectively. He also broke a number of American records. But plans for the same rider to attack Mike Hailwood's one-hour record of 144mph (232km/h) set on an MV Agusta at Daytona in 1964, were axed when Goodyear could not guarantee that their tyres would last sixty minutes.

Sadly, Kawasaki hopes of beating the existing twenty-four-hour record using stock Z1s just failed – even though one set a marginally *quicker* speed, both machines averaged over 100mph (160km/h). The faster set 109.64mph (176.41km/h), which, although an improvement, was not a big enough one to be accepted as a new record. This had been set at 109.23mph (175.75km/h) by a British BMW team on a modified 600cc R69S at the bumpy Monthléry circuit in France during 1961.

The fastest Z1 was ridden by Americans Cook Neilson and Hurley Wilvert of America, Englishman Cliff Carr and Masahiro Wada of Japan.

*Dave Aldana with another of the specially prepared Yoshimura Z1s at Daytona.*

*The fastest Z1 was ridden by Americans Cook Nielson (shown) and Hurley Wilvert, Englishman Cliff Carr and Masahiro Wada of Japan.*

*One of the Z1s
hurtling around the
Daytona banking.*

*The American magazine* Motorcyclist *sponsored this Z1 record bid at Daytona in
March 1973.*

*Several Z1s were raced in production machines' races, including this one seen at Snetterton in 1975 . . .*

*. . . and another at Brands Hatch the same year.*

Less obvious improvements were to the frame which benefited from heavier gauge tubing and other more minor changes. The battery was also mounted lower, whilst the gearing was raised by dropping two teeth on the rear wheel sprocket. Finally there were some small electrical changes, including the addition of a three-fuse system as used on some other Kawasaki models at that time, and an audible turn signal device. The same year a custom model, the Z900-B1 (more commonly known as the Z900LTD), was introduced (this is covered in Chapter 9).

Also worth mentioning are the various police models (in both 900 and 750 engine sizes), used in several countries including Japan and the USA; and the various specials which were built and marketed with Z1/Z900 power units. Notably these included the Rickman Z1 CR and the Read Titan Z1, both in the popular café racer mould. Paul Dunstall also got into the act, offering what the American magazine *Motorcyclist* termed the '*Zee Whizz*', using a Dunstall-tuned 1,100cc Z1-based engine producing 88bhp and an extra 10mph (15km/h).

At the end of 1976 the original '900' came to an end, Kawasaki stretching the motor to a litre; and so a new chapter in the four-cylinder story was about to unfold.

*The four-cylinder Kawasaki engine was also a popular choice with the straightline brigade. Here, Terry Revill is pictured with the Dixon Racing, twin-engined 1,800cc dragster in the late 1970s.*

## Z1 Scoops the Awards

Journalists all around the world fell for the Z1's combination of power, sophistication and modern looks: for its day, there wasn't another *mass*-produced streetbike to compare with the big, bold Kawasaki. The result was that the Z1 was voted for by the press and public alike in unprecedented numbers. This happened wherever the bike was sold, in both the specialist press and national newspaper contests. In fact, everyone and his dog seemed to be falling over backwards to give Kawasaki officials silverware of all descriptions. For example that top selling motorcycle newspaper, *Motor Cycle News* had up till then almost always seen their reader 'Machine of the Year' poll awarded to a British bike; but in 1973 the Z1 simply blitzed the opposition in the *MCN* contest. This trend continued even when the Z900 replaced the Z1!

Not to be outdone, *MCN*'s rivals, *Motor Cycle*, held their own 'beauty contest' in 1974. After the Z1 again took the honours, the newspaper had a special scroll prepared which was presented to Kawasaki. It read, 'This scroll is presented to Kawasaki UK Ltd on behalf of the readers of *Motor Cycle* who voted the 900cc four-cylinder Kawasaki Z1 "Superbike 1974" in our first contest of this kind. One in eight of the total vote entry from Britain and fourteen other countries chose the Z1 as the most desirable road bike in production.'

*Kawasaki Motors UK's Mick Uchida (in saddle) being presented with the 'Machine of the Year' trophy by* Motor Cycle News's *Peter Strong.*

*Not to be outdone, MCN's rivals* Motor Cycle *held their own contest in 1974 – it was won by the Z1, of course. The scroll shown here was presented to Kawasaki.*

### Frame-up: The Superbike Specials

In many ways the Superbike Special was a direct follow-on to the café racer of the 1960s. During the early 1970s there emerged a huge array of series production machines – led by the Z1 – in which bike manufacturers from around the world designed and built large capacity, relatively expensive 'Superbikes'. Manufacturers included Honda, Kawasaki and Suzuki (Yamaha would join in later); Ducati, Moto Guzzi, Laverda, Benelli, BMW and Harley-Davidson. One would have thought that ranged against the might of names such as those above, and with such a formidable array of engineering talent and models, the limited-production specialists would not have stood a chance. But for a variety of reasons, such was not the case.

*The Rickman CR café racer turned the stock Z1 into a sleek sportster.*

*The American magazine called it the 'Zee Whizz': the 1975 Dunstall-Kawasaki 1100 with 99bhp on tap.*

*Essex dealers Warnell came up with this rather tasty frame kit for road or track use. Power was provided by a suitably tuned Z1 motor.*

For one thing, there was then, as there has always been, a select number of people who desired to own something truly unique. Then there was the saga of the Japanese bikes which didn't handle, whilst the Italian industry shot itself in the foot by building some truly memorable bikes which had lousy chrome and paintwork. And finally, there was the fact that the major manufacturers always had to keep one eye on the increasingly vociferous 'green lobby', with the result that, as the 1970s progressed, many machines became overloaded with environmental hardware.

Into this arena came a plethora of names which flourished in this environment, including Dunstall, Seeley, Rickman, Bimota, Warnell and Harris. Dunstall, Rickman and Bimota all built Kawasaki-engined Superbikes with the support of the Japanese company, including a full Kawasaki manufacturer's warranty. And although some builders chose engines other than the Z1-type motor for instance, Bimota with their KB2 550-engined model, most Superbike Specials with Kawasaki power plumped for the classic 900.

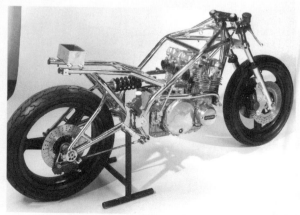

*One of the very first of the famous Harris frame kits was for the Z1/Z900 motor. Note the early form of monoshock rear suspension.*

# 4   After Z1

In late 1976 Kawasaki introduced its first 'small' four-cylinder machine, the 652cc (62 x 54mm) Z650. It not only set new standards in this capacity class, but was a truly great all-rounder, offering many of the virtues of much bigger machines but with substantially less weight and bulk, not to mention reduced running costs. In many ways it provided its owners with the benefits of the big bore Kawasaki fours, but with a lower initial purchase price, better fuel consump-

tion and potentially longer life from 'consumable' components such as tyres and drive chains.

Specification included electric start, five-speed gearbox, twin hydraulic front discs and rear drum brakes, 19in front, 18in rear wire (later cast alloy) wheels, and a duplex steel tubular frame. Over subsequent years it was to prove one of the best loved and most reliable Japanese motorcycles of all time. Production fully ceased in 1983.

*The Z1000 took over from the Z900 for 1977; here Prince Charles tries one for size in September that year.*

## Uni-Trak

Kawasaki's patented Uni-Trak rear suspension was developed over a relatively long period; indeed they were the first manufacturer to develop successfully a progressive rising-rate, single shock rear suspension system. Uni-Trak was first utilized on the prototype KR250 in-line twin road racer of 1976 – two years before Kork Ballington captured both the 250 and 350cc world championship titles on machines equipped with Uni-Trak rear suspension. The same rider repeated this test the year after (1979), and altogether KR250 and KR350 racers captured no less than eight titles before Kawasaki announced its retirement from GP racing, at the end of 1982.

In 1979, Kawasaki decided to make a serious attack on the 500cc motocross grand prix scene. They signed up the American ace Brad Lackey, and built a special bike for him – with Uni-Trak rear suspension. That year, he finished second in the world championships. Clearly the system worked, because what better testing grounds could there have been? The following year, customers could buy Uni-Trak motocross and enduro machines. The first production Uni-Trak roadster was the GP550 (factory code Z550H1) of 1982.

The system developed and fitted to the streetbikes benefited from the extensive competition developments, but was specially adapted for the particular needs of the street rider. Priorities were a progressive action which permitted very light and rapid suspension movements in response to minor road unevenness, while providing increasingly firm response to large road shocks. Kawasaki's engineers wanted – and got – first-class roadholding allied to greater rider comfort. The top of the shock absorber was attached to the lower part of the frame, the bottom being linked by a compound lever action to the swinging arm; being thus located, close to the machine's centre of gravity, increased handling stability. A leverage ratio of approximately 2:1 in the linkage meant that the speed of the shock absorber's movement was about half that of the swinging arm's causing very little heat build-up on the shock, and providing consistant damping.

While both spring pre-load and damping characteristics of the shock absorber might be varied (the method of adjustment varying between different models), the highly progressive control that the Uni-Trak system provided meant that frequent re-adjustment of suspension settings became a thing of the past.

By 1985, no less than fourteen Kawasaki roadsters were kitted out with the Uni-Trak system; these included the GPz1100, GPZ900R, GPZ750R, 750 Turbo, GPZ600R, GPz550 and the Z400F-11.

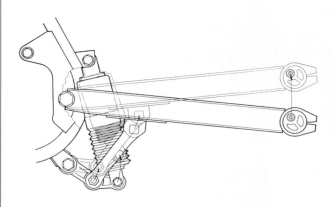

# uni·trak

*A revised version of Kawasaki's Uni-Trak single shock system, with the top end attached to the frame, and the bottom end linked by a compound-action lever to the swinging arm, was introduced for 1983. The models to use it included the GPz 750/1100, plus the 750 Turbo.*

*In December 1976,* Motorcyclist *magazine said: 'The new Z650 represents Kawasaki's best effort to date. Capable of running with the big tourers in a practical sense, it has excellent fuel efficiency and range. It is easy to service and overhaul and gets under the 750cc insurance premium!'*

In 1979, the four-cylinder theme was downsized further to provide the Z500. This 497cc (55 x 52.4mm) was also the basis for a successful one-model race series which was run in Britain during 1980; this was won by Neil Storey. An even smaller version, the Z400, also appeared with a 399cc (52 x 47mm) powerplant.

The first four-cylinder 750-class Kawasaki to sell on a world-wide basis was the 750E of 1980. Maximum power from the 738cc (66 x 54mm) engine was 79bhp, at 9,500rpm.

Meanwhile the 900 had grown to a 1000. This had been accomplished by the simple expedient of boring the cylinders out by 4mm to 70mm, giving a new capacity of 1,015cc. There was a wide range of models, including the Z1-R, Z1000ST, Z1000H, Z1000J and the Z1000R. The Z-1R was very much in the café racer mould, with its aggressive lines and colour-matched cockpit – there was also a choice of fuel tank size. The Z1000ST was in contrast a luxury touring mount with a plush specification which included shaft final drive. The Z1000H was Kawasaki's first production bike to feature fuel injection, whilst the J version was a budget-priced Superbike, and the R a road-going version of the sit-up-and-beg racers campaigned by the likes of Eddie Lawson or Wayne Rainey, so successful in the States during the early 1980s. Both riders were later to become world champions in the blue ribbon 500cc GP category, albeit not on Kawasaki machinery.

---

### Anti-Dive Forks

Before the advent of the latest generation of upside-down, cartridge-type front forks, several Japanese manufacturers used what were known as anti-dive-forks. An anti-dive system was employed by many four-cylinder Kawasakis of the 1980s to prevent excessive front suspension compression under heavy braking, permitting later braking without loss of control when entering corners at speed, and giving increased stability during emergency stops.

The Kawasaki system utilized a variable control valve in the hydraulic damping system of one, or both, front fork legs. When the front brake was applied, the rise in hydraulic pressure in the brake line was fed to the control valves in the anti-dive unit. As braking pressure increased, the control valve restricted the flow of oil in the forks, preventing excessive fork compression.

In practice, the telescopic forks functioned normally in response to road surface variations, but prevented the front suspension from over-reacting during sudden braking. An adjustment screw permitted the rider to select the level of anti-dive required.

In 1985 eight Kawasaki models featured anti-dive, including the GPz1100, GPZ900R, 750 Turbo, GPZ750R, GPZ600R and the GPz550.

---

By 1981 the Kawasaki four-cylinder range had grown to include the 553cc (58 x 52.4mm) Z550 and the 1,089cc (72.5 x 66mm) Z1100, the latter featuring shaft final drive.

For 1982 the GP range was introduced in 550, 750 and 1100 format, the latter with digital fuel injection (DFI) and chain final drive (it should also be noted that the Z1100 tourer continued as a separate model in its own right). The most important without doubt was the 550, which was not only a class leader, but also the first Kawasaki streetbike to feature Uni-Trak rear suspension, derived from the company's successful racing and motocross machines. Other notable features on the 1982 550GP included 61bhp, equalized, air-adjustable front suspension, bikini fairing, LCD readout for the instrument

*By 1980 the Z650 had gained seven-spoke alloy wheels, but the rightness of its design meant there was little need for much other change. Production was finally discontinued in 1983.*

It's the supersports version of the King Kawasaki Z1000 tuned for extra performance. And it will be the fulfillment of your ambition to own the most brilliant performance motorcycle on the market today. Give it a test ride and know what the top bike is all about.

90 hp, 1015 cc, DOHC, 4-into-1 exhaust, super styling, cast wheels

**Kawasaki**   DEALER NAME AND ADDRESS

*The 1,015cc Z1-R was the performance model in the 1978 Kawasaki line-up; maximum power was 90bhp at 8,000rpm.*

*Smoking the rear tyre for extra grip on the drag strip.*

*Nigel Patrick's turbocharged Maitland Kawasaki – the fastest petrol-burning bike outside the USA during the late 1970s – quarter of a mile (just under fikm) in 9.44 seconds, and a zero to 150.46mph 286.78km/h) speed.*

*This Z1-R based dragster was capable of a mind-blowing performance.*

*The flamboyant Japanese Moriwaki rider Masaki Tukuno.*

*The Moriwaki squad in the pre-race pit area at Daytona.*

*Tukuno, Moriwaki Kawasaki, Daytona 1980.*

*Dutchman Henk Vink at Santa Pod, 5 May 1980.*

## Kawasaki Electronic Fuel Injection (KEFI)

Although it was largely the Germans who had pioneered the use of fuel injection some years earlier, Kawasaki were to be amongst the first to get a system in a series production vehicle – in their case the Z1000H in 1980. Having the grand-sounding name of Kawasaki electronic fuel injection (KEFI), the system took the place of conventional carburettors and provided an electronically controlled fuel/air mixture to the engine. The system operated on the principle of continuous direct air-flow measurement to determine the correct fuel/air mixture.

Sensors in the KEFI system continually monitored engine speed and temperature, and intake air flow and temperature. The data was sent to the electronic control unit, which processed these signals and determined the fuel requirements of the engine. The control unit then generated an electrical signal which was sent to the fuel injector valves. The electro-magnetic injection valves opened and injected the precise amount of fuel needed in front of the intake valves. The injector valves' nozzles were designed to deliver a finely atomized fuel charge, which promoted even and complete combustion.

*The Z1000H was Kawasaki's first production streetbike to employ fuel injection in 1980.*

The KEFI had three basic components: an air intake system; a fuel delivery system; and an electronic control system. Its benefits included a superior cold start performance, improved fuel economy, lower exhaust emissions and lower maintenance. But this early system was replaced by the later digital fuel injection (DFI) which was pioneered on the GPz1100 in 1983, before being used on other Kawasaki models, including the six-cylinder Z1300.

The DFI was a much superior system, and is described in detail in Chapter 6. Nevertheless, KEFI charted the way both to Kawasaki and rival manufacturers, of just how important fuel injection would be in the future.

*Close-up of the Kawasaki electronic fuel injection (KEFI) system on the Z1000H.*

*The Daytona production racing class of 1980. Masaki Tukano (317) leads the field.*

panel, new five-spoke cast alloy wheels, forged aluminium handlebars and an oil cooler. There was also a six-speed gearbox.

The following year, 1983, Kawasaki produced a master marketing coup with the GPz range, incorporating 550, 750 and 1100 versions. These narrow focus sportsters – together with a 750 Turbo version which went on sale in 1984 – were the pinnacle of Kawasaki's air-cooled four-cylinder models. Each represented class-leading performance for its day: the 550 – 61bhp, the 750 – 86bhp, the 1100 – 120bhp and the 750 Turbo – 112bhp.

Testing the range-topping GPz1100 in the June 1983 issue of *Motorcycle Enthusiast*, Brian Crichton was definitely under the big Kawasaki's spell, starting off by saying: 'Yes indeed, sweet dreams are made of this. Mind-blowing power, superb stoppers, excellent

handling, a functional fairing and dynamic looks . . . all for a list price of £2,899.'

Compared with the 1982 1100GP, the 1983 1100GPz featured what is best described as a 'tuned' motor with an extra 11bhp of go. The official factory workshop manual for the 1983 1100GPz even devoted a two-page appendix to 'additional considerations for racing'. The ZX1100-A1 (to give it the official Kawasaki service designation) differed from the 1982 B2 model in several ways. The cams were lumpier, both giving 0.8mm additional lift and 12 degrees more duration: the lift was now 9.5mm and duration 300 degrees. Valves were larger: the 38mm inlet by 1mm, and the 32.5mm exhaust by 0.5mm, and the valve springs were stiffer to manage them. The angle of the exhaust valve had been steepened by a degree from 31.5 to 30.5mm from vertical, to complement what was

*Neil Storey, winner of the Z500 race series held in Britain during 1980.*

*Another Kawasaki rider at Daytona in 1980 was Eddie Lawson, later to become a multi-world 500cc champion. He retired his Moriwaki-prepared machine after 81 miles (130km) of the 200 (322km)!*

*An even smaller Kawasaki four, the Z400, also appeared at the same time (1980): 399cc (52 x 47mm).*

*The four-cylinder theme downsized to provide the Z500 (497cc – 55 x 52.4mm).*

*Late in 1980 the Z500 became the Z550 by simply increasing the bore size from 55 to 58mm, giving a new capacity of 553cc. This is a 1983 GPz550, with triple disc brakes and Uni-Trak rear suspension.*

*The 1983 GPz1100 with digital fuel injection (DFI). Pushing out 120bhp, it achieved 150mph (240km/h) in a Cycle magazine test; at that time the fastest streetbike they had ever ridden.*

*Loosely based on Eddie Lawson's American Superbike-winning racer, the 1984 Z1100R.*

*Expressly built for touring, the shaft drive Z1100A was a supremely comfortable bike which also found a niche with sidecar enthusiasts.*

described as a 'poluspheric' combustion chamber. In place of the previous hemispherical design, the new chamber shape was more like two small hemispheres side by side and, judging by Kawasaki diagrams, the GPz1100 head featured broader squish bands. The chamber was reduced in volume by 2.4cc and coupled with higher dome pistons, compression was up from 8.9 to 9.5:1. To help performance the inlet tracts were hand-ported for more efficient flow. The con-rods were stronger, the gudgeon pins were increased in diameter from 17 to 18mm, the transmission cogs undercut to reduce the possibility of jumping out of gear, spark advance was now electronic instead of mechanical, and the fuel injection system improved. The injector 'brain' was located under the seat tail. This automatically cut the fuel supply off if the engine was revved beyond 11,000rpm. The new digital system could compensate for changes in barometric pressure, and it did away with the air-flow

gate on the original system, thus providing an unrestricted passage to incoming air.

Brian Crichton achieved a best one-way speed of 139.64mph (224.68km/h). At 224kg (538lb) the GPz1100 was certainly no lightweight, but by the standards of the day it handled as well as any other Japanese 1-litre-plus machine – thanks in no small measure to the Uni-Trak system which was a revision from that fitted to the 550, and the three-way anti-dive front forks.

But just around the corner was a new era in motorcycling when there would be even faster bikes with smaller engines, uprated brakes, and of lighter weight. This new breed arrived in 1984 and was headed by Kawasaki's GPZ900R (see Chapter 10), the Suzuki GSX-R750 and Yamaha's FZ750. It would then be left to the venerable air-cooled motor to make way for this modern technology, before making something of a comeback in the form of the Zephyr retro bike (see Chapter 15) in the next decade.

## Kawasaki UK, the Early Years

How does a huge industrial organization such as Kawasaki Heavy Industries market its motorcycles? Here's how it went about establishing itself on the British market. 1974 saw Mick Uchida and Kit Kitayama arrive in Britain, expressly charged with getting Kawasaki sales moving, since these had suffered after a less-than-impressive four years with the Nottingham-based Agrati organization who also handled the distribution of Italian Garelli mopeds. Uchida and Kitayama therefore set up Kawasaki Motors (UK) Ltd, and the newly formed company began trading initially from the Holiday Inn, Marble Arch. Soon offices were acquired at Staines, with a parts warehouse at nearby Bedfont. With the first few dealers appointed (five of which, Avon Motorcycles, R W Parkinson, Cradley Kawasaki, Pegasus and Doug Hacking Motorcycles, survive at the time of writing), the first machine delivered by KMUK was on 13 May.

In a year which saw the Z1 Superbike voted *MCN* 'Machine of the Year' for the second year in succession, a total of 1,230 machines were sold from fifteen dealers, representing just over 1 per cent of the market (excluding mopeds). By the end of 1975 the dealer network had expanded to fifty solus dealers selling a six model roadster range, and three newly introduced off-road bikes. Once again the Z1 was voted top bike in the *MCN* poll. And with Mick Grant winning the Senior TT and Kawasakis finishing first, second and third in the Bol d'Or, UK sales went up to 5,500 with market share up to 3 per cent.

By the beginning of 1976 the company had outgrown its Staines base and re-located to a newer, larger premises in Slough. Once again the Z1 topped *MCN*'s poll. There were twelve roadsters in the range and over 11,000 units were sold – 10,000 more than two years before! And market share was 5.9 per cent. In 1977 the one hundredth dealer was appointed, the new Z650 and Z1000 were introduced, and the factory scored its first ever 250cc GP victory in the Dutch TT at Assen. And the following year saw Kawasaki become 250 and 350 world road racing champions, with Grant winning the Classic TT at 114.3mph (183.90km/h). On the sales front the Z250 Scorpion was introduced, the first model built expressly for the UK market. The company sold 13,000 machines and had 7.5 per cent market share.

1979 was a year of innovation, both as regards the model range *and* the dealer network. New models included the mighty Z1300, the Z1000ST, Z1000 Mk2 and the first middleweight four, the Z500. Kawasaki retained both the 250 and 350cc world titles, and by the end of the year over 15,000 bikes had left the dealers' showrooms. *But* the most significant news on the trade front concerned the creation of the 'B' dealer network. This was a distinct change in marketing policy, as from early days sales chief John Norman had promoted Kawasaki as a solus dealership; in the new system the original network supplied a much larger number of sub-dealers and was supposed to give the company a significantly increased market share. Not everyone in its solus network agreed, however, and several considered they had been bypassed by Kawasaki in its quest for a bigger market share.

In 1980 the UK market recorded its second highest ever sales peak; and with its new set-up, Kawasaki was well poised to take maximum advantage of this. It had several new models, the most important being the new 550cc which became a best seller. By now the roadster range had shot up to twenty-nine models, including the less-than-successful 550 and 750 LTD custom bikes. Nearly 22,000 machines were sold, resulting in the company breaking the 10 per cent market share barrier for the first time.

As history shows, 1981 proved a critical year for the industry. But KMUK were either very capable or very lucky, as they had not been drawn into the vast overstocking situation which led to widespread discounting and the financial suicide which certain other Japanese importers had created by their 'sales at all costs' policies over the previous couple of years. Unlike Honda and Yamaha in particular, Kawasaki had the advantage of a sensible stock level, and this helped their dealers to avoid at least some of the disastrous price war which engulfed the trade that year. They also introduced some important models, like their first sports mopeds (AR and AE50), the GPz sports concept and a new generation Z1000/1100 engine. One of the company's few mistakes in 1981 was not being able to introduce a water-cooled motocrosser, like its competitors, for the all-important schoolboy 125cc class in the dirt bike sector.

With the other Japanese manufacturers suffering from the chaos caused by vast overstocking, Kawasaki was able to use to full advantage its sensible stock levels. By the middle of 1982 they had the three top selling bikes over 500cc in Britain: the GPz550 (now with Uni-Trak rear suspension), the GPz1100 and the GPz750. In addition the shaft drive touring GT750, which had made its debut at the Milan Show the previous November, had come on stream and was selling well. Come 1983, and the level of success increased, with new versions of the GPz750 and 1100, the 750 Turbo and the sporting GPZ305. And a new 'who can catch Kawasaki' ad line was introduced. To cap an excellent year the GPz1100 was voted 'Machine of the Year' by *MCN*.

If 1983 seemed good, then 1984 was even better for the Slough-based company. Armed now with the new GPZ900R, Kawasaki dominated the over 500cc sales league, and their market share (including step-thrus) had increased to a healthy 13.5 per cent. The year ended with yet another victory in *MCN*'s poll, this time with the GPZ900R.

*Mr Tazaki (director and deputy senior general manager of Kawasaki Heavy Industries) signs the 'Big Red Book' at the twentieth anniversary celebration of Kawasaki Motors (UK) Ltd in spring 1994.*

Come 1985, and Kawasaki had ousted Suzuki from the number three spot for the first time ever and had a virtual monopoly on sales above 750cc. Not only this, but the GPZ900R was the UK's top selling machine over 125cc. Other items of interest that year included the launch of the GPZ600R and an electric start version of the KLR600 trail bike. The string of sales successes continued into 1986 with the appearance of the KMX125 which offered serious competition to the class-leading Yamaha DT125. At the opposite extreme, the GPZ1000RX and 1000GTR continued Kawasaki's lead in the muscle bike sector. In December the new GPX750 was launched. Other important developments that year included a special products division to concentrate on sales and marketing of non-motorcycle products, and a network of Jet Ski dealers was established. In addition, KMUK took over the distribution company previously responsible for warehousing and delivering bikes to dealers.

The rising value of the yen brought problems for the 'big four' in 1987, but even so Kawasaki still managed to increase its market share, thanks in no small way to bikes such as the recently introduced GPZ500S, a new higher performance twin, and the latest 600, the GPX.

And so for 1988, having suffered several years of decline, the industry finally began to show signs of recovery, with overall motorcycle sales (excluding mopeds) up by a total of 6.4 per cent while Kawasaki's sales increased by an impressive 15.6 per cent. By the end of the year, Kawasakis accounted for almost 20 per cent of the UK motorcycle market.

Behind these impressive figures were the real reasons: bikes such as the newly introduced ZX-10 voted 'Machine of the year' and perhaps more importantly, the top selling machine over 750cc with 1,060 units sold during 1988.

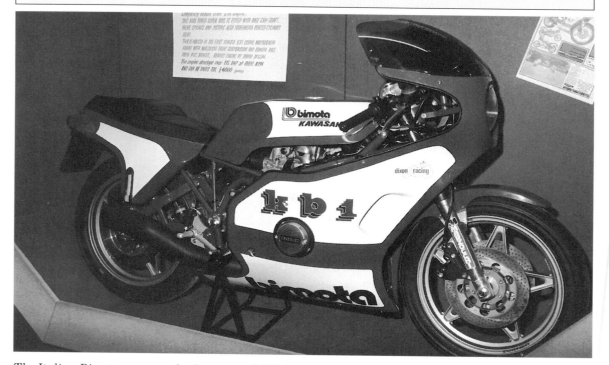

*The Italian Bimota company had a successful liaison with Kawasaki during the late 1970s and early 1980s. This produced the Z1-R engined KB1 (shown) and the later KB2, with the smaller GPz550 engine.*

*Not to be outdone,
the Swiss Moko
concern built a
series of Kawasaki-
engined Superbikes,
using their own
specially crafted
monoshock chassis.*

*British-built Harris
Magnum 2. Once
again Kawasaki
was the chosen
powerplant. The
year was 1982.*

# 5 The GT Series

Kawasaki's exotic sportsters might grab the headlines, but their less glamorous touring relations are the unsung heroes of the range; and none more so than the long-running and successful GT series.

The Milan Show is only held every two years, unlike most of its counterparts, and provides a fascinating window not just into the domestic motorcycle industry, but also for manufacturers from around the world. The 1981 show was no exception, with a host of new models and updated machinery. For a start, no less than sixty-eight different Italian bike-builders were displaying their wares, to which could be added another dozen or so frame specialists. Then add the other foreign exhibitors, and you have the most comprehensive and important motorcycle show on earth.

Into this hotbed of activity strode Kawasaki with their world title-winning endurance racer and Anton Mang's GP250

*Launched at the Milan Show in November 1981, the GT750 was a machine for enthusiasts who wanted a powerful, low-maintenance, shaft-driven tourer with less bulk than its one-litre counterparts.*

## Model: Z750GT P1 (1982) Europe

**Engine**

| | |
|---|---|
| Type: | Four-stroke, four-cylinder, air-cooled, dohc |
| Displacement: | 738cc |
| Bore and stroke: | 66 x 54mm |
| Compression ratio: | 9.5:1 |
| Ignition: | Transistorized |
| Starting: | Electric |
| Lubrication: | Wet Sump |
| Carburettor: | Mikuni BS34 x 4 |
| Spark plug: | Denso W24 ES-U/NGK B8ES |
| Exhaust: | Four-into-two |

**Transmission**

| | |
|---|---|
| Type: | Five-speed, constant mesh, return shift |
| Clutch: | Wet, multi-plate |
| Primary reduction ratio: | 2.550 |
| Gear ratios: | 1st 2.333; 2nd 1.631; 3rd 1.272, 4th 1.040; 5th 0.875. |
| Final reduction ratio: | 2.522 |
| Overall reduction ratio: | 5.629 |
| Final drive: | Shaft |

*The GT750 was to prove a best seller for one-and-a-half decades, its conservative styling and shaft final drive proving popular attractions down through the years. This example is being put through its paces in March 1982.*

## Model: Z750GT P1 (1982) Europe (Cont'd)

**Frame**
| | |
|---|---|
| Type: | Tubular steel, double cradle |
| Suspension: | Front: telescopic fork; rear: swinging arm |
| Tyres: | Front: 100/90-19 57H; rear: 120/90-18 65H |
| Wheels: | Cast alloy |
| Castor: | 27.5 degrees |
| Trail: | 104mm |

**Brakes**
| | |
|---|---|
| Front: | Dual 270mm disc |
| Rear: | Single 270mm disc |

**Electrical**
| | |
|---|---|
| Battery: | 12v 14ah |
| Headlamp: | 12v 60/55w |
| Tail/brake lamp: | 12v 5/21w x 2 |

**Dimensions**
| | |
|---|---|
| Length: | 2,255mm (88.78in) |
| Width: | 760mm (29.92in) |
| Height: | 1,105mm (43.50in) |
| Wheelbase: | 1,480mm (58.26in) |
| Seat height: | 800mm (31.50in) |
| Ground clearance: | 150mm (5.90in) |
| Dry weight: | 220kg (485lb) |
| Fuel tank capacity: | 24.3 litres (5.5gal) |

**Performance**
| | |
|---|---|
| Maximum horsepower: | 78bhp at 9,500rpm |
| Maximum torque: | 6.4 kg-m at 7,500rpm |
| Acceleration: | SS 400m (¼ mile) 12.3sec |
| Maximum speed: | 127mph (204km/h) |

rubbing noses with the less successful KR500 two-stroke four-cylinder GP racer and the prototype Z750T announced earlier at the Tokyo Show. But more important than all these interesting exhibits was the arrival of a new concept for the company, the GT: the Grand Touring 750. The newcomer was Kawasaki's response to the growing interest in touring bikes. And the emphasis of the GT was for more mid-range power and torque, a rubber-mounted engine, shaft drive for low maintenance and long-distance reliability, air-adjustable front and rear suspension, plus tapered roller swinging arm and steering head bearings for improved handling performance and durability.

Kawasaki's design team had as its priority a grand touring model with enough power to maintain high speed cruising with excellent reliability, handling and stability. At the heart of the machine was the 738cc (66 × 54mm) dohc air-cooled four, first used on the Z750 sports chain-drive tourer. This was tuned to provide a useful 78bhp. Other details of the power unit included a compression ratio of 9.5:1 transistorized ignition, electric start, five-speed gearbox, oil cooler, rack-and-pinion clutch release, 'silent' cam chain with automatic tensioner, and four Mikuki BS34 CV carbs. Compared with other touring machines of the same engine size, the GT750 was relatively light at 220kg (485lb).

Other notable items of the bike specification were three 270mm brake discs, each with a dual piston caliper employing sintered metal pads for consistent all-weather efficiency (something rival Japanese manufacturers were still struggling with at the time), front and rear suspension with rubber gaiters, a powerful rectangular quartz halogen 60/55W headlamp, dual horns, forged aluminium stubby handlebars, self-cancelling turn signals, and a new instrument panel with LCD display for major functions such as fuel, oil, battery and side stand warning. The tachometer also functioned as a voltmeter, there was a one-touch trip meter, also tubeless tyres (19in front, 18in rear), comfortable dual-density seat, aluminium rear carrier, two helmet locks, dog-leg levers, 'black rear light with two bulbs for extra safety', plus centre and side stands. And finally a black and gold finish: described in detail, 'Metallic Sonic Gold' was applied to the wheels, mudguards, tank, side panels and carrier, whilst a shiny black finish was specified for the 4-into-2 exhaust, fuel-tank cap and chassis components. Most of the engine was in the same style, but there was a black wrinkle finish on the cam covers and carburettor tops. 'Candy Wine Red' was available in place of the gold as an option.

*The easy-to-read instrument console of the GT750 – note the tacho/volt and trip reset buttons.*

*Three-tier oil cooler . . .*

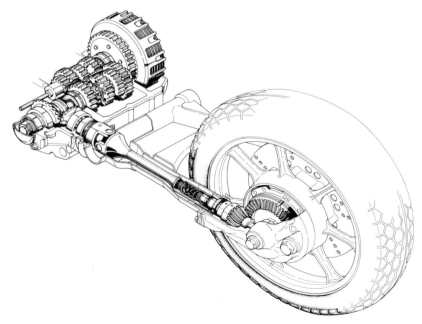

*. . . and shaft final drive details.*

Although it could almost be labelled a 'plain Jane' bike, the GT concept seemed to hit all the right notes with buyers, who voted Kawasaki's new machine a winner with their wallets. This excellent reception led directly to the launch of the GT550 just over a year later. With a dry weight of 201kg (443lb) it was lighter than its bigger brother, although of course its 553cc (58 x 52.4mm) GPz550-based motor was also significantly less powerful, both in terms of maximum output (56bhp at 9,000rpm) and torque. However, it was ultimately to prove even more popular than the 750, the main reason being its suitability for despatch rider duties

– it was to replace Honda's CX500 V-twin as *the* despatcher's bike on the city streets of Europe.

Of course there were changes besides the cubic capacity of the engine: smaller, less powerful brakes (a pair of 242mm discs at the front, and a 180mm drum at the rear); a six- instead of five-speed gearbox; and a smaller capacity oil cooler, for example. However, both GTs offered smooth, generally vibe-free (thanks to rubber-mounting), plush air suspension and a well padded seat (which was stiff as a board on delivery, but eased off as the miles passed to provide a very reason- able degree of luxury). All they really lacked

*The 1992 version of the GT750 was readily identifiable by its all-blue colour scheme with gold pin-striping, a more classic (Z!) look for the familiar four-cylinder engine. Less obvious was a change to Keihin CVK 32 carbs which boosted mid-range power.*

*The smaller GT550 arrived in time for the 1993 season. This is the original G1 model, which like the early GT750 had an all-black engine and exhaust.*

was a fairing to shield the tiring wind-blast for out-of-town use, and a pair of panniers to provide carrying capacity. Several owners fitted the latter, but few fairing-equipped GTs were ever seen. The effects of the shaft final drive were barely noticeable, thanks to a special drive-line shock absorber.

The frame on both GTs was a straightforward tubular steel cradle unit, and compared with many modern machines with smaller diameter 16 or 17in wheels, the front end of both models appeared a touch ponderous on the steering at low speeds. One side product of this was excellent high speed, straight line stability, even fairly strong cross-winds having little effect on either GT model. With large capacity fuel tanks – the 750 at 24.3 litres (5.5 gals) and the 550 at 21.5 litres (4.25 gals), the range varied between 185–220 miles (298–354km) on both bikes.

For two-up use the larger machine is more suitable. Although not totally underpowered, the 550 does lack punch low down, and can leave you wanting more, particularly when two-up. However, once revving it feels strong

enough, and it is happy to cruise at 90mph (145km/h) as long as your arms will pull against the wind blast. The top speed of the 550 is 112mph (180km/h), whereas the 750 will be good for almost 125mph (200km/h).

The year 1984 saw both GTs have much of the black chrome finish of the engine units deleted, and with bright chrome finish for the exhaust system they looked far less austere than when launched. The 550, now code G2, also benefited from electronic advance and a safety side stand, as did the 750, coded P3. And as if to prove the rightness of the original concept, nothing else had been changed.

And except for a minor update of the smaller GT for the 1991 season (launched in October 1990), that was really it. The 550 was by now coded G7, and its changes consisted of an intake silencer added to help reduce intake noise; carburettors changed from CV30 to Keihan CVK30; and the same type of cylinder head as the Zephyr retro installed. There was also a new colour – 'Candy Persimmon Red' to give potential

*In October 1990 Kawasaki launched the G7 version of its smaller GT. This had a number of changes, consisting of an intake silencer, carbs changed from CV to CVK 30 Keihins, a new top from the recently introduced Zephyr, and a new colour option of Candy Persimmon Red.*

*New top end engine styling.*

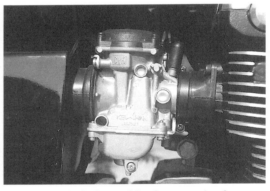

*Leading axle forks and brakes remained unchanged.*

*CVK instead of CV carbs.*

*As did the useful cast-alloy rear carrier . . .*

*. . . lockable fuel filler . . .*

*. . . excellent switchgear . . .*

*. . . and air-adjustable rear shocks.*

buyers an option from luminous 'Polaris Blue'.

Besides its niche market as just about the ideal despatch rider's machine, the GT has also built up a loyal non-specialist following: it even boasts an owner's club expressly for these eminently practical, unsung heroes of the bike world. Both are still in production, but from the end of 1996 only the 550 was still imported in the UK. Without doubt those machines must hold something of a record for length of production and the least number of changes during this period of any modern motorcycle – certainly as regards the Japanese variety.

*Despatch rider Steve Jones with his GT750, on which he had clocked up well over 200,000 miles (321,800km) when this photograph was taken in August 1990.*

*GT750s on 'duty' during the 1984 Milk Race, a cycle race around Britain which was staged annually during the summer months.*

# 6    The Z1300 Six

The mighty six-cylinder Z1300 ran for almost a decade; it was also one of a trio of prestigious Superbike sixes of the late 1970s and early 1980s, the other two being designs from Honda and the Italian Benelli factory. Although it could hardly be described as pretty, it was nonetheless an extremely sophisticated piece of technical wizardry. Even the engine layout, behind a vast radiator, did nothing to enhance its aesthetic qualities. The sheer bulk of the Z1300 is proven by its 294kg (653lb) dry weight, which has only been exceeded by Honda's Gold Wing and Harley Davidson's Electra Glide; however, both these machines feature comprehensive fairings and luggage systems, whereas the Z1300 was all pure, naked muscle.

One person who proved just what was possible – or not – on one of the Japanese giants was the Finnish stunt rider Archie Nyquist, who amazed crowds all over Europe with some truly amazing feats on his Z1300. Archie pulled wheelies as if he were mounted on a dirt bike, whilst his speciality was to get his Z1300 up to 100mph (160km/h), then *step off* and be pulled along behind!

The first the world saw of what was to be labelled 'King Kawasaki' was at the International Cologne Show in West

*The truly awe-inspiring six-cylinder Z1300 was launched in December 1978. It was destined to remain in production for almost a decade before being finally killed off in mid-1988.*

*Stunt rider Archie Nyquist proved that the Z1300 could be coaxed into doing just about anything.*

Germany on 23 September 1978, some five years after first consideration to the design had been given. The prototype model displayed on Kawasaki's stand was covered by a simple black sheet. A large gathering of motorcycle journalists from around the world, together with enthusiastic first-day visitors, crowded around, and when the cover was finally removed, there was a hushed silence. The audience was awe-struck. No doubt about it, the machine really did impress at first sight – and continued to hold the assembled crowd's attention for a long time as the various parts of the Z1300's components were studied in detail. Kawasaki's response to the hyper-Superbike challenge had been bold and strong.

At first glance the Z1300 didn't look quite what one would have expected of a mighty six-cylinder water-cooled (remember the Benelli and Honda were air-cooled!) machine. Its totally integrated design, with a relatively low seat height and cleverly contoured tank, deceived the eye into

*The liquid-cooled 1,286cc six-cylinder, dohc transverse engine, together with its final drive system.*

## Model: Z1300 A1 (1979) Europe

**Engine**

| | |
|---|---|
| Type: | Four-stroke, six-cylinder, water-cooled, dohc |
| Displacement: | 1,286cc |
| Bore and stroke: | 62 x 71mm |
| Compression ratio: | 9.9:1 |
| Ignition: | Battery and coil, full transistor ignition |
| Starting: | Electric |
| Lubrication: | Wet-sump |
| Carburettor: | Mikuni BSW32 x 3 |
| Spark plug: | Denso/NGK BR8ES |
| Exhaust: | Six into two |

**Transmission**

| | |
|---|---|
| Type: | Five-speed, constant mesh, return shift |
| Clutch: | Wet, multi-plate |
| Primary reduction ratio: | 2.651 |
| Gear ratios: | 1st 2.294; 2nd 1.667; 3rd 1.280; 4th 1.074; 5th 0.931 |
| Final reduction ratio: | 4.546 top gear |
| Final drive: | Shaft |

**Frame**

| | |
|---|---|
| Type: | Tubular steel, double cradle |
| Suspension: | Front: telescopic fork; rear: swinging arm |
| Tyres: | Front: 110/90V–18; rear: 130/90V–17 |
| Wheels: | Cast alloy |
| Trail: | 102mm |

**Brakes**

| | |
|---|---|
| Front: | Dual 260mm disc |
| Rear: | Single 250mm disc |

**Electrical**

| | |
|---|---|
| Battery: | 12v 20ah |
| Headlamp: | 12v 60/55W |
| Tail/brake lamp: | 12v 5/21w x 2 |

**Dimensions**

| | |
|---|---|
| Length: | 2,332mm (91.81in) |
| Width: | 836mm (32.91in) |
| Height: | 1,155mm (45.47in) |
| Wheelbase: | 1,587mm (62.48in) |
| Seat height: | 810mm (31.89in) |
| Ground clearance: | 142mm (5.59in) |
| Dry weight: | 296kg (652.6lb) |
| Fuel tank capacity: | 25 litres (5.5gal) |

**Performance**

| Maximum horsepower: | 120bhp at 8,000rpm |
|---|---|
| Maximum torque: | 11.8kg-m at 6,500rpm |
| Acceleration: | SS 400m (¼ mile) 12.0sec |
| Maximum speed: | 140mph (225km/h) |

*The sheer size of the Z1300 is evident in this shot, its 294kg (653lb) dry weight only beaten by Honda's Gold Wing and Harley-Davidson's ElectraGlide.*

believing the machine was smaller than it actually was; but close up, you quickly realized this was a no-nonsense touring sportsbike which fully deserved its 'King' title. The slab-sided engine and fuel tank were massive, but everything else – wheels, tyres, leading axle forks, rectangular headlight, brakes, instruments – were all in proportion and blended together as a single, harmonious unit.

The across-the-frame, water-cooled engine was conventional, with typically Japanese-type horizontally split crankcases and separate block and head. Displacing 1,286cc – and in an effort to keep overall engine width to a minimum – the crank was of the long-stroke type with bore and stroke dimensions of 62 and 71mm respectively. Compared to Honda's CBX, the Z1300 was a full 80mm narrower at the cylinder head, and 60mm narrower at the cylinder block.

Kawasaki's engineering team decided at an early stage to go for a straightforward double overhead camshaft design with two valves per cylinder to help reduce weight and maintenance costs – the four valves per cylinder they thought was just too much at that stage. The six exhaust pipes exited the cylinder head and tucked behind the radiator to converge into two pipes with a connection

*Cutaway of Z1300 showing some of the design details.*

pre-chamber and into separate three-in-one mufflers, one each side of the machine.

The water-cooled concept was included from the onset to give the 'Super Z' a more refined quality image whilst providing greater reliability, durability and development potential. The narrow water jackets reduced mechanical noise by a considerable degree and allowed the engine to operate more efficiently in a better controlled temperature range than if it had been air-cooled. It was also the company's first production water-cooled motorcycle engine.

Carburation was taken care of by a trio of 32mm CV (constant velocity) double-barrelled Mikunis specially developed for the Z1300. A set of three twin throat units instead of six carburettors meant reduced width, and the rider's knees would have a more natural grip of the tank – in other words, a more comfortable riding stance. Smooth running was achieved by having one cylinder firing every 120 degrees of the crankshaft revolution. This meant less vibration, besides which the fundamental 'motorcycle' characteristic was retained. You were always aware of having plenty of power on tap if required.

In line with achieving a 'good citizen' image Kawasaki continued its PCV (positive crankcase ventilation) system, like its other four-stroke machines. The PCV system recycled unburned blow-by gases through the carbs and this markedly reduced emissions

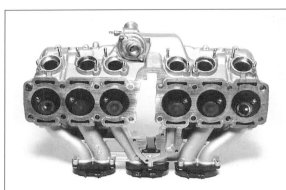

*Cylinder head.*

*Crankshaft.*

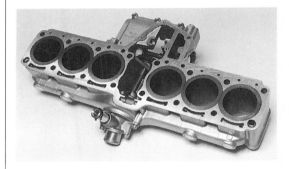

*Cylinder barrel.*

*Connecting rod assembly.*

*Camshafts, valves and cam chain.*

*Piston.*

*Clutch.*

*Oil pump.*

*Oil pump internals.*

*Drive shaft.*

*Rear bevel box.*

for a cleaner exhaust, without incurring any loss of power.

To emphasize its sports-touring image, Kawasaki equipped its range topper with shaft drive – this was located on the offside of the machine and allowed the footpegs to be perfectly equal and in line. The system adopted was unique when introduced with two additional spring-loaded, metal-to-metal shock absorbers integrated in the crankcase and lubricated by engine oil and featuring tapered roller bearings for the shaft itself. Kawasaki also claimed that if anything went wrong it would be less expensive to fix than other systems.

For the top bike in its range, Kawasaki loaded its six cylinder with the very best instruments and equipment. The large, square-shaped headlamp had a powerful, penetrating halogen beam, and the turn signals featured specially designed lenses which were brighter when illuminated and therefore more visible, providing greater safety. In addition, there were twin double-tone horns located up front with a clear and commanding warning. Switches and handlebar controls were upgraded, whilst the instruments were newly designed in a squared panel which housed the massive speedometer, tachometer, water tempera-ture and electric fuel gauge, together with the usual array of warning lamps.

The electrical specification of the machine was equally impressive, the Z1300 having a maintenance-free full transistor ignition system and a heavy-duty 12v 20ah battery; electric start was standard, as it was by now in the vast majority of Japanese machines – if not by then those of European origin. The ignition key was used for other functions, for example to unlock the separate, spring-loaded section of the side panel, and the seat could then be lifted up to reveal a toolbox and small hidden compartment in the squared-off tail section in which could be

carried essential papers and other small items.

The dual-level seat itself was deeply cush-ioned and contoured to give the rider as low a riding position as possible, and the passenger extra comfort on the slightly raised rear section. It is worth noting that most riders of average height would be able to straddle the big six and still have both feet firmly planted on the ground for full support.

As for the frame, this was designed for additional strength and rigidity, with larger diameter tubing than was to be found on other Kawasaki large capacity machines such as the Z1 and Z1000. For example the double cradle downtubes were of 34mm (1³/₈ in) diameter (Z1000 - 31.8mm) and the walls were 2.3mm thick. The steering head section and swinging arm were specially gusseted to maintain stable handling under all possible conditions. Lighter gauge tubing was utilized on non-load-bearing sections in order to achieve sensible weight limits, and a specially patented construction of double-wall section downtube was employed near the head for added strength. The swinging arm had double needle roller bearings.

The front forks were provided with a leading axle which permitted a longer stroke and softer spring rate; this in turn meant a more comfortable ride which combined with extra capacity rear shocks. Even when fully loaded with touring gear and a passenger, the Z1300 still gave predictable handling characteristics to generate confidence and ensure a relaxed ride.

Double 260mm disc brakes up front and a single 250mm disc at the rear took care of the stopping. The stainless steel discs were drilled to eliminate brake squeal and reduce weight, – although in all truth it must be said that these, together with the vast majority of motorcycle braking systems of the period, were considerably down on present-day standards.

## Air-Adjustable Suspension

Touring machines in particular can be subjected to widely varying loads, depending on whether the owner is riding solo, or is carrying a pillion passenger plus a load of luggage. The variation between laden and unladen weights can be really quite extreme.

In the early 1980s, when most large capacity touring models still had twin rear shocks, Kawasaki introduced (in 1983 on the Z1300, plus the GT550/750 and Z1100) air-adjustable units. These permitted the rider to alter the rear suspension quickly and easily so as to compensate for the change in load, and to enable the machine to be set to suit the preferred characteristics. By using air as the spring medium, any increase or decrease in 'spring rate' was infinite, and not restricted to a number of fixed settings.

With the Kawasaki system, the air-adjustable shock absorbers featured an equalizing tube which connected left- and right-hand units, so that air pressures were perfectly matched in each unit. This ensured that there was no suspension imbalance (this could adversely affect handling) and that adjustment was very simple: air was either added (or removed) via a single valve. The company also equipped several of its larger capacity machines (including the Z1300) with single inflation point, air front forks during the same era.

Air under compression can be made to function extremely well as a spring, with the attractive bonus that it can be readily adjusted to suit one's requirements. When used as a supplementary spring medium in the front forks, air provides very smooth cushioning – and that in turn means that the tyres maintain improved contact with the road surface. By using an equalizer tube to inter-link both the fork legs, a single inflation point could be utilized to increase/decrease operating pressures, and at the same time ensure that the pressures in each leg were perfectly matched.

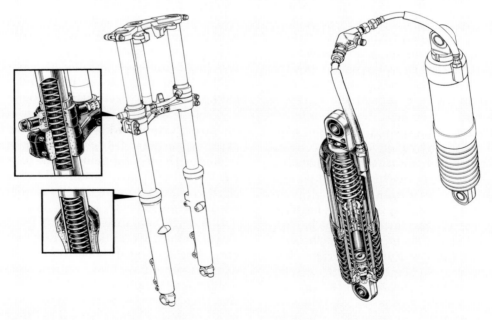

*Air-adjustable front and rear suspension was a factor of the Z1300, signalling its luxury touring role.*

*The French Jewell
sidecar and the
Z1300 made a first
class combination,
1983.*

But in many ways the Z1300 was a pioneer: it was one of the very first production motorcycles to use wide-section tubeless tyres – 110/90Vx 18 front and 130/90V x 17 rear; self-cancelling turn signals; the extra power and security of a dual-bulb rear lamp (with an indicator lamp in the instrument panel to warn of failure); and finally, more than a thousand different ignition key combinations to reduce the possibility of theft.

Launched towards the end of 1978, the Z1300 went on sale in January 1979, production lasting some ten years before finally ending in 1988. There were surprisingly few major changes along the way from the original 1979 Z1300A1 through to the final ZG1300G3 of 1988. The maximum speed of the original 1979 model was 130mph (210km/h) – providing, of course, that you could hold onto the beast at this velocity, as Kawasaki had omitted to provide its Big King with any sort of fairing.

For the 1980 model the prefix was changed to A2, but the only difference was in colour choice. For 1981 the A3 model gained adjustable air rear shocks, while the 1982 A4 featured transistorized ignition with electronic advance.

Little change was made for the A5 of 1983, but 1984 saw the Z1300G1: this had digital fuel injection (DFI), which had been pioneered on the 1100 the previous year. The DFI system replaced the three double choke, constant velocity Mikuni carburettors. Compared with the more conventional electronic fuel injection (EFI), the DFI has no flaps or gate to measure the air flow, which leaves the intake passage completely unobstructed and thus free from the turbulence created by such sensors. Even more importantly, it eliminates the slight hesitation which occurs between the opening of the throttle and the response of the air flap to the increased air flow. The system

*Rear end details of
Kawasaki's six,
including cast
alloy wheel, shaft
final drive, pillion
footrest and rear
shock.*

eliminates the tendency for the air flap to
bounce when the throttle is closed and then
immediately snap open again – this can
cause a sudden delay just when immediate
acceleration is most required. In place of the
EFI system's restrictive air sensor, the DFI
reads the throttle opening, engine revs, air
and engine temperature plus the atmos-
phere pressure. It then instantaneously
computes the appropriate fuel injection rate
for optimum performance.

The digital fuel injection system also has a
'fail-safe' circuit which allows the motorcycle
to be ridden even if the electrics pack up.
Other advantages of the DFI are smoother
and more immediate throttle response,
easier starting (regardless of engine
temperature) and significantly improved
high altitude performance (the altitude
sensor can even register changes in the barometric pressure due to the weather). Fuel
consumption and exhaust emissions are also
improved.

In 1986 the G1 became the G2, but with no
actual changes. The final year of the big Z
was 1988, by which time the model had

changed yet again, to the G3. By this time it
had been in production for almost a decade,
and while motorcycle design and production
techniques had gone forward at a breathtaking pace, the basic design and styling
of the six-cylinder Kawasaki had remained
virtually unaltered. The result was extinc-
tion for a bike which, although never built in
vast numbers, had nonetheless created its
own niche in the market place as the ultimate heavyweight sports tourer. Only its
lack of weather protection as standard equipment had spoiled an otherwise impeccable
record. Many owners saw it as a real classic
amongst machines conceived in the 1970s –
in the days before the advent of the race-
replica plastic rocket ship it was hi-tech, but
of a different generation to bikes of the 1980s
and 1990s.

Road-testers' opinions of the Kawasaki
giant seemed to differ very little, which is
quite unusual. Most appeared surprised at
just how easy it was to control, and discov-
ered it was not the cumbersome oil tanker
that most had feared. Although very much a
sports tourer, the Z1300 would happily pull

*Dominant would be one way of describing the Z1300.*

*Little and Large – guess which one is the Z1300? The top box and panniers probably outweigh the neighbouring scooterette.*

from as low as 800rpm in top, up to its 8,000rpm redline with virtually no hesitation or strain at all. The combination of six cylinders, water-cooling and shaft drive provided not only a unique, but a very smooth and sophisticated means of two-wheeled travel. Add to this a reasonable level of handling and braking combined with supreme comfort, and one had a motorcycle capable of travelling long distances – its only real failing being the amount of wind intrusion due to no form of fairing.

# 7  Turbo

As the 1980s dawned, the world's bike builders viewed the turbocharger as a way to create a relatively lightweight machine that could be both docile yet dominant. But what seemed a relatively easy task turned out to be exactly the reverse, and no manufacturer achieved that goal in the first round of development, including Kawasaki. The only difference was that the other factories put their turbos on the market, whereas 'Big K' put theirs back on the drawing board.

From the beginning Kawasaki decided that its turbobike would adhere to well known guidelines, and would follow function – with the functions being top performance, predictable operation and high reliability.

*The 750 Turbo project started off in 1980 as a 650. To improve both torque and speed it was decided, in spring 1981, to base the bike on the GPz750. And after abandoning the original long induction system, the Kawasaki effort was to emerge as the most successful of the Japanese turbo-bikes of the early 1980s.*

These were the Kawasaki trademarks established by such previous classics as the Z1, and rather than compromise the design (which happened with Honda, Yamaha and Suzuki), Kawasaki stuck to the guideline until the original goal had been achieved. The result was to be a streetbike like no other: a *successful* factory-built turbo motorcycle.

The project started in 1980 as a 650. A prototype was track-tested in January 1981, with results that would have placed it comfortably ahead of the then-current 650-based turbobikes: 100bhp, a maximum speed of 141mph (227km/h) and a 400m (¼ mile) time of 11.3 seconds. To improve low-speed torque and long-term reliability, it was decided in the spring of 1981 to base the bike on the normally aspired GPz750. Testing during that summer led the engineering team to abandon the original long induction system – with a two-compartment airbox – and move the air filter to the nearside of the engine. Meanwhile, Hitachi introduced a new high-performance turbocharger which was selected for the redesigned machine.

The next prototype, with a half fairing, was displayed at the Tokyo Show in November 1981. Extensive wind-tunnel testing had revealed that the fairing needed to be redesigned for better performance. Further testing yielded the final production

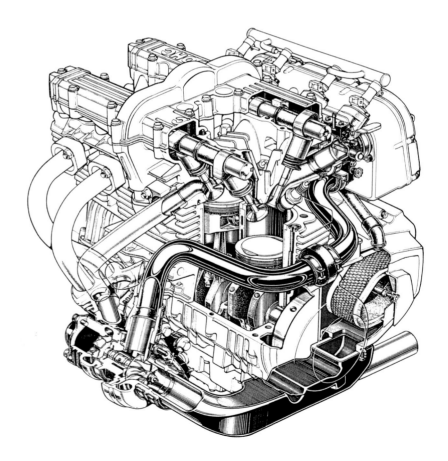

*By placing the turbocharger as close as possible to the exhaust ports, Kawasaki's engineers greatly reduced turbo lag. Note the air filter close to the gearbox sprocket to shorten the induction path and again reduce turbo lag.*

## Specification

| | |
|---|---|
| Model name | 750 Turbo, year 1984 |
| Marketing code | ZX750-E1 |
| Engine type | Turbocharged, four-stroke, four-cylinder, dohc |
| Displacement | 738cc |
| Bore and stroke | 66 x 54mm |
| Ignition system | Transistorized, electronic advance |
| Fuel system | Digital fuel injection (DFI) and turbocharger |
| Transmission | Five-speed, wet multi-plate clutch |
| Suspension | Front: adjustable air fork with equalizer |
| | Rear: Uni-Trak (air) |
| Tyres | Front: Michelin 110/90 V18 tubeless |
| | Rear: Michelin 130/80 V18 tubeless |
| Braking system | Front: dual disc |
| | Rear: single disc |
| Seat height | 780mm (30.7in) |
| Dry weight | 233kg (514lb) |
| Fuel tank capacity | 17 litres (3.75 gal) |
| Max power | 112bhp at 9,000rpm |
| Max torque | 10.1kg/m at 6,500rpm |

component, first with an integrated frame member and up to that time the most efficient from an aerodynamical standard. Meanwhile, all other components of the bike were being thoroughly tested and honed to produce what was to prove a remarkably sound motorcycle right from the outset.

The outstanding feature of the design was the unique placement of the turbocharger in *front* of the engine, and as close as possible to the exhaust ports. This position is best from a performance standpoint, but presented a variety of complex engineering problems, such as routing four exhaust pipes to the turbo collector in a very small space.

Comparing the standard GPz model with the turbo, at first glance it was difficult to tell them apart, but after the turbo installation the other giveaway was an aluminium section in the middle of the fairing. This was actually a specially designed brace which

was there to give the frame additional rigidity and help protect the turbocharger from damage. Using the 1983 GPz750 as a base, the 750 Turbo went on sale in early 1984. Besides the addition of the turbocharger and related equipment, modifications included the following:

*Engine*: Cylinder head from Z650, with laminated stainless steel gasket. Shorter duration and less cam lift than GPz750. Flat-top pistons with thicker sidewalls. Lower compression ratio. Digital fuel injection. Reduced venturi inner diameter at throttle valve. Increased main oil pump capacity (17 per cent). Primary shaft-driven scavenging pump to draw oil to crankcase from turbocharger. Inline oil filter ahead of turbocharger.

*Transmission*: All new gearing. Tempered primary chain.

*Clutch*: Additional plate and strengthened hub.

*One of the GPz750 Turbos (coded ZX750E1) at its European launch in Austria during the spring of 1984.*

*Frame*: New assembly of large diameter, thin wall tubing in configuration similar to GPz1100. Longer steering head than GPz750. Frame-mounted full fairing with aluminium cross-frame member and under-cowl. Stronger aluminium box swinging arm (wall thicker by 0.5mm).

*Dimensions*: Weight increase due to addition of full fairing and strengthening components. Lower seat.

*Suspension*: New initial set length and decreased stroke front and rear. Higher spring constant and more progressive linkage on rear only.

*Brakes*: Discs and calipers from GPz1100. Anti-dive units improved (lowest setting equals GPz750's highest setting).

*Tyres:* V-rated Michelin tubeless type. Many features of the GPz750 were retained, including:

- Basic engine
- Four-tier oil cooler
- Silent cam chain with automatic tensioner
- Air-adjustable, equalized fork up front, and four-way adjustable rebound damping plus air-adjustable preload at rear.

## KAWASAKI TURBO SYSTEM

The purpose of a turbocharger is to make use of the large amount of energy carried away by exhaust gas. This energy, readily avail-

*Close-fitting exhaust pluming.*

*Not to be outdone, Kent-based Mortimer Engineering created their own Kawasaki Turbo – but this was based on the earlier Z1000. Seen here at the Racing Show, Alexandria Palace, London, February 1984.*

able when an engine is under load and exhaust flow is high, is used to force a higher volume of air through the engine, increasing its effective displacement. Thus turbocharging delivers extra power from an engine in the middle and high rpm ranges. The general advantages of this are obvious; in that a given amount of power can be extracted from a relatively small, light engine, and when extra power isn't needed, it can be run economically at relatively low rpm.

Japan's motorcycle factories applied turbocharging in different ways – from simple to ultra-complex – with mixed results.

Suzuki and Yamaha placed turbos behind their across-the-frame four-cylinder engines, which made routing of the exhaust pipes relatively easy but had the disadvantage of increasing response time because the turbo was some considerable distance from the exhaust ports. Meanwhile Honda placed the turbo near the exhaust ports of its CX V-twin models but high in the frame, which contributed to an already high centre of gravity.

To combat turbo lag, some manufacturers (including several in the auto industry) have used reed intake valves to bypass the turbo

*750 Turbo control layout; simple when compared to its Honda, Suzuki and Yamaha rivals.*

until boost pressure surpasses atmospheric pressure. The intention is to let the engines run efficiently without boost, but because of relatively low compression ratios, power output is still less than it would be with non-turbocharged engines. But Kawasaki engineers went a stage further. To eliminate the low-rpm bypass found on early Kawasaki prototypes, and to enhance response time further, the company's engineers shortened the induction path as much as possible by placing the air filter near the engine sprocket (this was done without affecting the bank angle). The result of their work was shown by four positive outcomes: first, minimal lag between the time the exhaust gas leaves the ports and starts driving the turbine; second, minimal loss of heat energy in the turbo system; third, a relatively low centre of

gravity; and fourth, heat isolated from the rider.

The Kawasaki turbocharging system was protected by a wastegate which passed exhaust gas around the turbo if boost pressure reached 560mmHg. As a further safety measure, the DFI system cut off fuel supply to the engine if boost reached dangerous levels. As a rider aid, the LCD boost gauge was fitted in easy view on top of the tachometer. For those who wanted to race the bike without the standard air filtration system, the compressor wheel was specially treated to withstand increased abrasion from unfiltered air.

Of vital importance, as with any turbo, were regular oil changes, and the procedure of allowing the engine to run while stationary at tickover for some thirty seconds

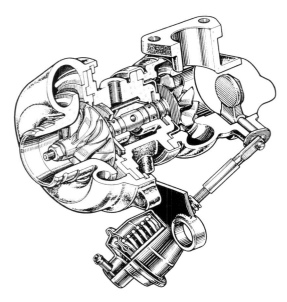

*The purpose of a turbocharger is to make use of a large amount of energy carried away by exhaust gas. This is the Kawasaki unit.*

before turning off the ignition. As for performance, Kawasaki claimed 112bhp at 9,000rpm, 10.1kg/m of torque at 6,500rpm, a maximum speed of 147mph (237km/h) and 400m in 10.9 seconds. By 1984 standards this was very quick; added to this, the 750 Turbo weighed some 11kg (24lb) less than the company's GPz1100, and from 3.3 to 13.3kg (7.3 to 29.3lb) less than the other Japanese turbos.

## MOTORCYCLE ENTHUSIAST ROAD TEST JUNE 1984, BY MICK WALKER

### Kawasaki ZX750E-1 Turbo

When I tested Suzuki's turbo, the XN85, it left a lasting impression of being an underrated motorcycle, with 1-litre Superbike performance above 5,500rpm, coupled with good handling and flickability on back roads or roundabouts, qualities which do not usually come with the normal run-of-the-mill Japanese Superbikes.

Kawasaki's turbo was all that I expected and even more, and its performance and handling combined produced something very special. Strangely it has been left to Suzuki and now Kawasaki to deliver the goods after both Honda and Yamaha failed miserably – in fact the Yamaha turbo is probably the ugliest motorcycle currently available! Kawasaki's brochure on the ZX750 goes so far as to quote, 'The 750 Turbo is the closest thing to perfection we've ever built.' In the real world just how true is this statement?

Kawasaki engineers had one main theme with their turbo: to produce a 750 with the power of an 1100. This called for a production streetbike to out-perform the opposition, a motorcycle that would be docile about town, but dominant out on the open road.

Right from the first moment I sat astride the turbo and pressed the starter button I felt comfortable and part of the bike, a good feeling, which was heightened when moving off. The dog-leg levers made control easy, and in coping with the Oxford traffic I found the motor both flexible and docile at low rpm. What finally settled any original doubts I had that the bike was one for the open road only came with the surprising realization that both feet could be put flat down on the road when at a standstill. I soon realized the true advantages of a well designed turbo: tremendous performance, coupled with a much superior power-to-weight ratio, a strange mixture of docility and fire dependent on whether you are on or off the turbo.

Before taking the Kawasaki from Oxford Motorcycle Engineers showroom I had a chat with fellow enthusiast, Simon Esnouf, who together with his wife had been impressed with a ride on the turbo. He considered that

*Whilst the 1984 Lotus Esprit Turbo produced more bhp per litre than any other production car, the Kawasaki 750 Turbo bettered this by more than 50 per cent.*

the reasons for making the ZX750E-1 his next bike were performance, racy style, the reliability record of Kawasaki's engines, and the price, compared to bikes of similar performance.

After leaving the crowded streets of Oxford I quickly found the machine changed its character as the mood suited, and that its performance when it was pushed hard was stunning. Here is a motorcycle for the experienced rider: it has a large reserve of power available, but in the hands of an in-experienced rider I could well imagine that it would be too fast for its own good. This is not to say that the bike is dangerous but it undoubtedly calls for respect.

One of the bike's few faults was that it is all too easy to touch the horn button when intending to use the flasher or indicator switch; this is embarrassing, if nothing else. Except for this the switches and instrumentation could not be faulted, and if compared to those on the Suzuki turbo were simpler and more basic.

The riding position was just as good at high speed as when ridden in city traffic. To complement the dog-leg control levers, the adjustable clip-ons suited the position, and the screen deflects the air satisfactorily. The fairing is similar to the swoppy affair found on the GPz range, but with an alloy section incorporated. It tucks in around the engine unit very neatly, and the mirrors were not affected by the usual blur.

The one area where I felt the Kawasaki failed to achieve the expected level of quality was in some of its cycle-part components. For example, whereas the Suzuki has

## Racing a Turbo

Although turbocharged cars have been used in Formula 1 racing in modern times, the FIM had banned their use in motorcycle grand prix events after the war. So you might assume that nobody in the bike world has raced a turbo for the last half century – but you would be wrong! At least one such machine was ridden to many a victory during the mid-1980s. Stranger still, it was via a British Italian bike specialist!

*This almost standard turbo was successfully raced in the mid-1980s by North Leicester Motorcycles. Rider Dave Humpstone (seated) broke several lap records for the production class.*

North Leicester Motorcycles have long been one of the UK's leading Moto Morini dealers, but at that time also sold Kawasakis. Stuart Mayhew, one of the NLM bosses, was largely the driving force behind the story. He had a passion for Italian machinery, but could also recognize that, in the 750 Turbo, Kawasaki had a machine of special merit. He believed it would be seen as 'a true classic in the years to come, revered with Vincent, Velocette and Ducati'. So the seeds of a dream to race a 750 Turbo were born. NLM had the facilities: a rolling road, dynamometer, gas analyses, plus mechanics fresh from Kawasaki factory courses on fuel injection and turbocharging.

Through a succession of events, Stuart Mayhew ended up loaning Dave 'Sooty' Humpstone a 750 Turbo, as it was noticed that the ACU production racing rule book allowed either a 750cc turbocharged or normally asperated 1,100cc engine in their regulations at that time. Dave Humpstone was a racer of some experience, and amongst other machines had successfully campaigned a Z1000J Kwacker, on which he had secured a number of wins. This included holding a couple of lap records. But he had also had his fair share of crashes, including quite nasty ones at

Cadwell Park and Darley Moor. NLM's turbo team first appeared on the scene in the summer of 1985, on the 22 June at Cadwell Park to be precise. The results were certainly encouraging to the team, if not the opposition, with a win, a second and a third. Next day at Darley Moor it was second, third and another second. Then a return to Cadwell the following weekend brought another victory and more leaderboard placings; and on the 14 July at Darley Moor came no less than three victories in three starts.

This last meeting had seen a disappointing practice session before racing got under way, besides a risk of the unknown, as it was very much a case of using untried gearing. Having drawn a start at the rear of the grid, Dave Humpstone had wound the bike up and dropped the clutch – with the result that the front wheel was soon up around his ears. Nothing daunted he carried on, changing gear and avoiding competitors who loomed up under him. One of his chief fans, Mick Francis, invented a new dance in his excitement watching the wheelying spectacle – by the first corner Dave had lowered the front wheel to aid steering, and looked around: there was no one left in front of him, and he remained there throughout the race. Here was convention being turned on its head: big-bore proddie racing at that time meant making full use (and sometimes a shade more!) of the ACU's 1,100cc upper limit, so the arrival of the 750 Turbo and Dave Humpstone had been met with the

general opinion – from the rest of the paddock – that NLM were brave but foolish to enter such a bike. Then winning just seemed to bring excuses and the word 'luck'. Much later, however, the mood was to swing and those same competitors were murmuring that it was 'unfair' that a turbo should be allowed at all.

For a couple of seasons the NLM 750 Turbo was a major force in British racing at production class level, including the Metzeler Series. The team revelled in swimming against the tide – and the added bonus of winning on something different to the norm.

Finally, and really only to demonstrate the ability of its workshop (there was no doubting of Dave Humpstone's ability) NLM went racing with a Suzuki GSX-R1100, like everyone else. The team continued to do very well, but the magic had faded – and it was hardly good business for a Kawasaki dealer to race a Suzuki. So NLM gently withdrew from its track commitment, whilst Dave Humpstone pursued his living with heavy goods vehicles, racing now taking very much a back seat.

Perhaps the most amazing part of this story is just how standard the NLM 750 Turbo really was.

*Dave Humpstone taking the NLM 750 Turbo to one of three race victories at Darley Moor, 14 July 1985.*

polished forged alloy clip-ons and better looking wheels, the Kawasaki had steel, black-painted handlebars and rough-cast wheels. The Kawasaki paintwork was rather basic, and like most of their 1984 range there is hardly any brightwork, only black paint, plastic and contrasting red paint. It would appear that the money has been spent elsewhere, on the engine and chassis, and this certainly shows in the performance and handling, both of which are top notch.

I would give ten out of ten for performance, although handling and roadholding is spoilt by a slight tendency of 'white lining' at speeds of around 45mph (70km/h) – strangely only at this figure; higher or lower it was all right, so I would give this section nine out of ten. Tyres on the test bike were Michelins, M48 rear and A48 front.

At almost its maximum speed the turbo could not be induced to do anything untoward in the handling department. I found that the Kawasaki had a wider power spread than the Suzuki, and I do not consider this to be centred around the Kawasaki's larger capacity as this is minimal, the Suzuki being 683cc and the ZX 738cc, a difference of only 55cc. To illustrate this, it was quite practical to let the motor run down to 40mph (65km/h) in top, and still be able to pull away providing the throttle was used sensibly.

Externally many of the items used are stock GPz, and I'm convinced that this is where Kawasaki have scored in making their turbo an attractive machine price-wise at £2,899. One of the few unpainted alloy parts on the bike is surprisingly the swinging arm.

In fact I initially suspected this to be silver-painted steel in the best Japanese tradition, but not so, it was real alloy!

Whilst it is possible to say that the ZX750 is not quite as quick as the GPz1100 or Honda's CB1100R on absolute maximum speed, I believe it to be superior to any other road bike from, say, 60 to 100mph (100 to 160km/h). Certainly it produces more power between 3,500 and 7,300 rpm than either of its 1100 competitors. What is most important, mid-range power out on the road, or a couple of miles an hour above the 140 mark? Right, you have the answer. The ZX750 is the most usable big bike currently available from Japan, regardless of cubic capacity – but don't take my word for it, take a test ride yourself. It combines the lightness of a 750 with the power of an 1100. It's docility in town is matched by its super-quick racer stance out on the open road, it handles and stops, what else could you want?

Of course it's not perfect, but it is nearer than I would have thought possible before riding it. My only complaints are the confusion, at high speeds, between the buttons on the left-hand switch, the white lining at 45mph (72km/h) and the positioning of the choke lever, situated on the carburettor rather than in sight up on the handlebars. On a personal note, I felt that there was an over-abundance of black plastic, but at least it won't rust!

Truly the ZX750 Turbo rates the title 'and the last shall be first'; it even gets serious consideration for the title of finest road bike – and who would have thought a turbo might have got *that* tag a year ago? So much for progress!

## Comparison of Selected Turbo and GPz750 Specifications

| Engine | | | 750 Turbo | GPz750 | |
|---|---|---|---|---|---|
| Compression ratio: | | | 7.8:1 | 9.5:1 | |
| Carburetion | | | DFI | Carburettors | |
| Venturi diameter | | | 30mm | 34mm | |
| Spark plug | | | NGK BR9EV | NGK BR9ES/Denso | |
| | | | | Denso/W27ESR-U | |
| Valve timing | Inlet | Open | 22 BTDC | 38 BTDC | |
| | | Close | 52 ABDC | 68 ABDC | |
| | | Duration | 254 | 286 | |
| | Exhaust | Open | 60 BBDC | 68 BBDC | |
| | | Close | 20 ATDC | 38 ATDC | |
| | | Duration | 260 | 286 | |
| Cam profile | | In. lift | 7.5 | 8.5 | |
| | | Ex. lift | 7.5 | 8.5 | |
| | | | | | |
| **Transmission** | | | | | |
| Primary reduction ratio | | | 1.935 | 2.550 | |
| | | | (23/23x60/31) | (27/23x63/29) | |
| Gear ratios | | 1st | 2.285 (32/14) | 2.333 (35/15) | |
| | | 2nd | 1.647 (28/17) | 1.631 (31/19) | |
| | | 3rd | 1.272 (28/22) | 1.272 (28/22) | |
| | | 4th | 1.045 (23/22) | 1.040 (26/25) | |
| | | 5th | 0.833 (20/24 | 0.875 (21/24) | |
| Final reduction ratio | | | 3.066 (46/15) | 2.533 (38/15) | |
| Overall reduction ratio | | | 4.946 | 5.653 | |
| | | | | | |
| **Clutch** | | | | | |
| No. of plates | | | 8 | 7 | |
| | | | | | |
| **Dimensions** | | | | | |
| Seat height | | | 781 | 790 | |
| Dry weight | | | 233 | 219 | |
| Curb weight | | Front | 123 | 116 | |
| | | Rear | 131 | 122 | |
| | | | | | |
| **Suspension** | | | | | |
| **Front spring rate (kg/mm):** | | | | | |
| Initial set length (mm) | | | 40 | 35 | |
| Stroke (mm) | | | 130 | 150 | |
| **Rear spring rate (kg/mm):** | | | | | |
| Spring constant | | | 9.1 | 8.6 | |
| Initial set length | | | 9 | 10 | |
| Stroke (mm) | | | 60 | 65 | |
| | | | | | |
| **Brakes** | | | | | |
| Eff. dia. | | Front: | | 246 | 236 |
| | | Rear: | 236 | 226 | |
| | | | | | |
| **Tyres** | | | | | |
| Size | | Front: | 110/90 V18 | 110/90 V18 | |
| | | | Michelin A48 | Dunlop F17 | |
| | | Rear: | 130/80 V18 | 130/80 V18 | |
| | | | Michelin M48 | Dunlop K427 | |

# 8  Touring GTR Style

Launched in the spring of 1986, the 1000 GTR was Kawasaki's first purpose-built touring bike. Its natural competitor was BMW, most notably the four-cylinder K-series, and in particular the touring package K100RT model. Both the German machine and the GTR (known as Concours in USA) were expressly designed for the rider who wished to travel fast without sacrificing the comfort, convenience and load-carrying capacity of a large capacity touring machine. Big K's effort had one big advantage over the BMW: price. But even so, it was the equal of the German model on technical gizmos.

Essentially the GTR was a combination of a detuned GPZ1000RX powerplant, new diamond frame, shaft drive and radial tyres. The 997cc (74 x 58mm) double overhead camshaft GPZ1000RX-based motor was detuned to provide suitable characteristics

*Easy on the eye and eminently practical, the 1000GTR was Kawasaki's first purpose-built touring bike.*

for the task at hand, with five notable changes: airbox, smaller 32mm versions of the aluminium Keihin carburettors, smaller diameter 31.8 instead of 38.1mm CVKS as used on all GPZ models, and softer lift camshafts and valve exhaust header pipes.

Maximum power of the original A1 (Official factory coding, ZG 1000-A1) was 108.5bhp at 9,000rpm, with maximum torque being produced at 6,500rpm. Kawasaki claimed 135mph (217km/h) and the standing 400m (quarter mile) in a very acceptable twelve seconds. But some markets were not as lucky, Germany and Sweden being restricted to 100bhp, whilst the poor old Swiss had to do with a mere 70bhp. An oil cooler was, however, standard issue for everyone. To minimize torque reaction during high speed work, the shaft/swinging arm was exceptionally long –

528mm (20.8in) from pivot centre to axle centre.

Based on the frame used by the GPZ900R, the GTR's diamond assembly utilized the engine as a stressed member of the chassis. In this design, the downtubes are eliminated and the powerplant is mounted lower, thus not only cutting weight, but also providing a lower centre of gravity. This, at least in theory, should provide improved handling and less top weight; however, from the author's own personal experience of the GTR, don't expect sportsbike steering sharpness!

The one-piece main frame was constructed of high-tensile steel and consisted of steering head, backbone tubes, swinging arm pivot, and rear section support. A short bolt-on alloy rear section supported the dial seat and standard-fit panniers.

*The British police showed an early interest in the GTR for patrol work, but although impressed, decided to stick with their BMW K100s instead. The purchasing authorities had to follow a 'buy European first' policy.*

## Model: ZG1000 (GTR) A1 1986 (Europe)

**Engine**

| | | |
|---|---|---|
| Type | | Liquid-cooled, four-stroke, four-cylinder, dohc, 16-valve |
| Displacement | | 997cc |
| Bore and stroke | | 74.0 x 58.0mm |
| Compression ratio | | 10.2:1 |
| Ignition system | | Maintenance-free electronic |
| Starting system | | Electric |
| Lubrication system | | Forced lubrication (wet sump) |
| Engine oil | | SE SE or SF 10W40, 4 litres (7 pints) |
| Carburettor | | Keihin CVK32 x 4 |
| Spark plug | | NGK DR8ES or Denso X27ESR.U |
| Valve timing | Inlet: | Open: 37.5 degrees BTDC; close: 57.5 degrees ABDC |
| | Exhaust: | Open: 57.5 degrees BBDC; close: 37.5 degrees ATDC |
| Charging current and voltage (night time at 4,000 rpm) | | Voltage: 14.5V |
| | | Current: 14A |

**Transmission**

| | | |
|---|---|---|
| Final drive | | Shaft |
| Gearbox | | Six-speed return shift |
| Primary reduction ratio | | 1.732 (97/56) |
| Gear ratios | 1st: | 3.071 (43/14) |
| | 2nd: | 2.055 (37/18) |
| | 3rd: | 1.590 (35/22) |
| | 4th: | 1.333 (32/24) |
| | 5th: | 1.153 (30/26) |
| | 6th: | 0.965 (28/29) |
| Final reduction ratio | | 2.708 (16/21 x 32/9) |
| Overall reduction ratio | | 4.530 at top gear |
| Clutch | | Wet, multi-disc |

**Frame**

| | | |
|---|---|---|
| Type | | Tubular diamond frame |
| Suspension and wheel travel | Front: | Air-adjustable telescopic fork 140mm |
| | Rear: | Uni-Trak, 140mm |
| Tyre size, make and type | Front: | 110/80 VR18, Dunlop K105F, tubeless |
| | Rear: | 150/80 VR16, Dunlop K700G, tubeless |
| Tyre inflation | Front: | 2.5kg/cm$^2$ |
| | Rear: | Up to 97.5kg (215.5lb) load: 2.5kg/cm$^2$ |
| Castor (rake angle) | | 28.5 degrees |
| Trail | | 123mm |

**Brakes**

| | | |
|---|---|---|
| Front | | Dual discs, dia. 270mm |
| Rear | | Disc, dia. 280mm |
| Braking distance | | 12.5m at 80mph (125km/h) |

93

**Electrical equipment**

| | |
|---|---|
| Battery | 12V 18 AH |
| Headlight | 12V 60/55 W |
| Tail light | 12V 5/21 Wx2 |

**Dimensions**

| | | |
|---|---|---|
| Overall length | | 2,290mm (90in) |
| Overall width | | 760mm (30in) |
| Overall height | | 1,415mm (55.7in) |
| Wheelbase | | 1,555mm (61.22in) |
| Ground clearance | | 140mm (5.5m) |
| Seat height | | 815mm (32.08in) |
| Dry weight | | 258k (56.87sq.lb) |
| Curb weight | Front: | 142kg (313 lb) |
| | Rear: | 152kg (335 lb) |

**Fuel tank capacity**              28.5 litres (6.25 gals)

**Performance**

| | |
|---|---|
| Maximum power | 108.5bhp at 9,000rpm |
| Maximum torque | 10.0 kg.m/6,500rpm |
| SS 400m (¼ mile) | 12.0sec |

Colours                                    Candy Wine Red, Pearl Gentry Grey

*Although no sportsbike, the GTR could still provide stable handling for high speed work.*

*A line of thirteen GTRs during the staging of the 1989 national Milk Race. Over the years Kawasaki UK supplied a number of different models for this important task.*

The Dunlop radial tyres were the first of their type to be fitted to a standard production Kawasaki, offering improved stability at high speed over conventional tyres of the period.

Fitted as standard equipment, the large fairing provided a good measure of protection against the elements. The specification included a comprehensive screen, flush-mounted headlamp, integrated direction indicators, digital clock and two storage compartments.

A large, 28.5 litre (6.25 gal) fuel tank gave sufficient range for the serious touring buff, and a range of 300 miles (480km) could be achieved when a sedate riding stance was used.

Each pannier held up to 10kg (22lb) and could accommodate a full-face helmet. The panniers were removable in seconds by simply flipping a single latch, whilst the integral handles made them easy to carry when not on the bike. When the panniers were removed, special body panels were provided to cover the mounting points. There was what Kawasaki described as a mini-carrier which had a maximum of capacity of 5kg (11lb).

Air-adjustable Uni-Trak rear suspension featured four-way rebound damping, whilst at the front the air-assisted forks featured 41mm (1.6in) diameter stanchions, plus an equalizer for simpler adjustment.

The heavy duty 12-volt electrical system comprised a 400-watt alternator, electric starter, electronic ignition, 60/55-watt halogen headlamp and an 18-amp hour battery.

Braking was looked after by a pair of 270mm discs up front and a single 280mm unit at the rear, all with sintered metal pads. The six-spoke aluminium wheels had different sizes – an 18in at the front and a 16in at the rear, the latter being an attempt to provide a more friendly seat height – something which BMW's K100RT wasn't too clever at.

A number of official Kawasaki accessories were soon made available; these included a tote bag which could be strapped to the rear carrier or saddle, a two-part tank bag (which when used together provided 20 litres (4.5 gals) of carrying capacity), and pannier bags (designed to fit inside the pannier cases), the latter coming as standard equipment with the motorcycle.

As for colours and graphics, for the original A1 model there was a choice of 'Pearl Gentry Grey' or 'Candy Wine Red'.

*By 1989 the GTR was in the A3 prefix. But in truth, except for very minor changes, the model has been little altered through its long career.*

*Kawasaki's first four-cylinder streetbike, the legendary Z1, circa 1973.*

*The Z1 engine: 903cc (66 x 66mm), air-cooled, dohc, four-cylinder, four-stroke.*

*In late 1976 Kawasaki introduced their first small four-cylinder roadster, the Z650. This is a 1978 model with one of the factory's KR GP racers in the background.*

*One of the original 1979 Z1300 A1s, liquid-cooled six cylinders and shaft drive.*

*A 1982 Z1300 A4, the first year the model featured transistorized ignition with electronic advance.*

*Arto Nyquist, a stunt rider from Helsinki who thrilled crowds all over Europe during the early 1980s with his Z1300.*

*Kawasaki was the first Japanese manufacturer to build custom bikes; this is an LTD550 of 1980.*

*Launched at the Milan Show in November 1981, the GT750P1 went on sale in early 1982.*

*The first Kawasaki streetbike to feature Uni-Trak rear suspension was the GP550 of 1982.*

*Turbo installation on the 1984 750 gave far less lag than on its Honda, Yamaha and Suzuki rivals.*

*Eddie Lawson made his name on a series of air-cooled four-cylinder Kawasakis during the early 1980s.*

*The first of the liquid-cooled 600s, the GPZ A1, 1985.*

*A journalist putting one of the first GPZ900Rs (Ninja in the USA) through its paces at the Leguna Seca launch in early 1984.*

*Next came the GPZ 1000RX in 1986.*

*The Zephyr 550 which first appeared in 1990 (Japan and the USA) is largely credited with starting the retro craze.*

*Launched in the spring of 1986, the 1000GTR was Kawasaki's first purpose-built touring bike.*

*A 1992 Zephyr 1100A1 waiting for its owner to 'kit up' and go.*

*British champion John Reynolds with a ZXR 750 in 1992.*

*ZXR400-mounted Neil Baker was joint winner, with Scott Smart, of the 1994 British SuperTeen championship title. Neil's father Paul is seen here with the bike.*

*The ZX-6R Ninja appeared in 1995 to challenge Honda's CBR600 for sporting honours in this most important class.*

*The ZZ-R1100 (and ZZ-R600) were updated in 1993; this is a 1996 D4 version.*

*The ZX-9R did not hit it off first time, but the 1998 model shown features a significant redesign and is much improved.*

For 1988 the GTR received the A2 prefix; the following year saw the arrival of the A3 and for 1990 the GTR was sold in the A4 version. By 1993 the prefix was A8. But in technical terms the GTR remained virtually unchanged. What did change in this period were colour schemes, and these included 'Pearl Alpine White', 'Candy Persimmon Red', 'Luminous Polaris Blue' and even for a short period 'Dark Green'. The other virtually unnoticed change had been to fit an increasingly restrictive exhaust system which was to see the power output of the unrestricted market variant drop to a low of 84.5bhp by the 1992 season.

In September 1993 Kawasaki unveiled the A9. This featured new front suspension with conventional damping (the original air adjustment having been deleted) with pre-load adjusting. There was also a redesigned seat. A major improvement was to the braking system. In place of the original solid twin 270mm front discs came a pair of semi-floating 272mm components, whilst dual two-piston calipers replaced the original single piston type. The single 280mm solid rear disc remained unchanged.

The instruments were revised, with twin trip meters now being specified.

Another change was a new design of cast alloy wheel; there was also a new front mudguard, together with wider section front wheel (now 3.0 in place of 2.15). To match this there was also a fatter front tyre – up from 110/80 to 120/70 – but still 18in. Other changes included the fairing inner cowl (with two storage compartments) and new, improved switchgear. There were also revised colours and graphics, using differing colours on upper and lower fairings, there being a choice between 'Luminous Vintage Red' or 'Pearl Cosmic Grey'.

When first conceived Kawasaki envisaged a 'ten-year lifespan target'. This has been achieved, and at present the company has no plans to cease production, such has been its success and reliability record in service with customers all over the world. Its owners view it with affection as an *affordable* but serious touring machine, designed to be equally adept at cruising down the autostrada with a pillion and a stack of holiday luggage as it is threading through traffic chaos on the way to work in suburbia.

# 9 Custom Cruisers

Of the Japanese 'big four' motorcycle marques, it has often been Kawasaki that has been the originator of a particular niche creation; and no more so than in the field of the factory-built custom bike. The company was the first to appreciate – and meet – the demands for an off-the-peg custom motorcycle; a machine with all the looks, style and appeal of a chopper, but with the reliability, practicality and competitive price tag that only a major manufacturer can provide. It was also a route which Harley-Davidson had been following, and still follows to the present day, with notable success.

Back in 1974 the company established a new plant in Nebraska. This had manufac-

turing and assembly facilities and was known as the Kawasaki Motors Manufacturing Corporation, based in the town of Lincoln. Within six years from start-up it was able to boast that it was the largest motorcycle producer in the USA – including Harley-Davidson! A significant part of this success story was down to one motorcycle, the Z900 B1, or as it was more commonly known, the Z900 LTD; 'LTD' stood for 'Limited Edition', and it was the very first Japanese bike built in the custom mould. Built at the Lincoln Nebraska plant it had the further advantage of being able to carry a 'Made in USA' sticker, even though the engine unit was Japanese built.

*Kawasaki were the first of the Japanese bike builders to appreciate and meet the demand for an off-the-peg custom motorcycle. Their first model was the American-built Z900B (more commonly known as the Z900LTD) of 1976.*

*By 1980 there was a whole family of LTD four-cylinder custom cruisers, and the craze had spread to Europe, the range consisting of 550, 750 and 1000 models.*

The motor and transmission were stock 900 without any change, but fitted with a Stateside-manufactured Jardine four-into-two exhaust which terminated in a shallow megaphone-type muffler on each side of the machine. The frame retained the standard swinging arm, but was equipped with Mulholland shocks. Wheels were another change, with Morris cast aluminium featuring seven spokes and shod with Goodyear GT rubber. The front remained at the 900s standard 19in but there was now a fat 16in at the rear.

The brakes were another area of difference over its roadster brothers, with discs all round. The dual front discs were actually of slightly increased diameter (up from 296 to 300mm) whilst the thickness was reduced by 2mm. The calipers were reversed so that they were mounted at the rear instead of the front. This was actually a good move, and was adopted on later Kawasaki models, almost across the range. At the rear, a single disc was bolted to a new, smaller hub (the standard Z900 had a drum rear brake) which retained the sprocket cush drive housing from the roadster.

There were abbreviated, chrome-plated mudguards, whilst the instrument pods were also given the shiny treatment. Other differences included a smaller fuel tank, and a twin-tier dual seat with larger chrome grab rail. The bars were of the pull-back variety, whilst other styling changes saw modified side covers and a chrome-plated chainguard. The centre stand was deleted due to the new exhaust system, but the prop-stand remained.

In its first year of production (1976) Kawasaki built 2,000 Z900 LTDs and supply simply couldn't match demand. However, because it had promoted the *'Limited Edition'* tag, the company didn't feel able to meet this extra demand, so the many unsatisfied customers had no option but to wait until the following year. Of course, supply and demand being what they are in the capitalist world, the other Japanese manufacturers now jumped on the custom bandwagon – but at least Kawasaki had the satisfaction of being first.

By 1980 there was a whole family of LTD four-cylinder models, and the craze had spread to Europe, with the range now consisting of Z550 LTD, Z750 LTD and Z1000 LTD, plus the more lightly styled Z650 SR. At the top of the tree sat the Z1000 LTD, a machine which Kawasaki described as 'the ultimate trip for the custom enthusiast'. By this time the LTD series was firmly established as an integral part of Kawasaki's world-wide product range – even though the original idea had come from the American arm.

A major advantage of the Z1000 LTD was its relatively low weight of 234kg (516lb) some 10–15kg (22–33lb) less than rival models from other manufacturers. Another plus was its durable engine, shared with the Z1000J. This familiar 998cc (69.4 x 66mm) dohc four cylinder with two valves per cylinder was specially tuned to provide a wide power band and increased long-term reliability – both important to the potential custom-bike buyer. Maximum speed was a claimed 135mph (217km/h). To provide greater freedom from vibration, the Z1000 LTD sported rubber engine mounts, these proving particularly effective at isolating the high frequency vibes associated with fast engine speed, adding to more relaxed riding. A 'silent' cam chain with automatic tensioner and transistorized, breakerless ignition also helped the cause. All the instruments were electrically operated. Other notable features included: leading axle, air-adjustable front forks; seven-position pre-load rear shocks; self-cancelling turn signals; four-fuse electrical protection, stepped dual-density saddle, dual horns, two helmet locks, anti-hot wire security device, 'black' tail light, short dumpy twin megaphone-style mufflers with four exhaust pipes, triple 236mm drilled discs,

*The Z1000 LTD under test during 1981; plenty of chrome and polished alloy to keep shiny.*

*Next down from the one-litre LTD was the 750. This offered a good mixture of power, style, price and ease of handling.*

seven-spoke wheels (19in front, 16in rear), and a low 785mm (30.9in) seat height for the rider. There was also an abundance of bright chrome plate and polished alloy, which was great if you loved cleaning and polishing your pride and joy, or an absolute pig if you were lazy (dusty, dirty custom bikes certainly don't suit the image!).

At 211kg (465lb), the 738cc (66 x 54mm) Z750 LTD offered less for less, at a lower price: 74bhp, smaller triple 226mm discs, 124mph (200km/h), lower alternator output (down from 20A/14V at 8,000rpm to 17A/14V at 10,000rpm), a lower set height (770mm/30.3in) and a smaller fuel tank of 12.4 litres (2.75 gals) against 15l (3.25 gals) on the Z1000 LTD.

The smallest LTD four was the Z550, with its 553cc (58 x 52.4mm) yet cheaper cost and less performance and custom goodies. Its lower weight and cheaper insurance also attracted some customers.

The 652cc (62 x 54mm) Z650SR was a 'mild' custom, very much a toe-in-the-water job. Although mechanically similar to the Z650C and Z650F, it had a visually different identity, the intention being to attract someone who liked the idea of a custom bike, but didn't want to go as far as LTD styling. There were still the dumpy megaphone-type mufflers, the combination of thin front 19in and fat 16in rear tyres, and seven-spoke cast alloy wheels, but otherwise there were more conventional traits such as relatively flat,

*Pop singer Suzi Quatro with an LTD750 outside a Croydon theatre in May 1980.*

narrow bars; a lot less chrome plate, flatter dual seat, painted mudguards and a generally more restrained appearance.

By the mid-1980s yet more Kawasaki customs had arrived on the scene, including the VN750 and 1500 V-twins (the latter name Sumo in certain markets) and the ZL900 Eliminator four. This used a detuned version of the 908cc (72.5 x 55mm) engine first seen in the GPZ900R sports/tourer.

As if all this wasn't enough, in 1987 there was the ZL1000, of which *Cycle* magazine got excited enough to shout. 'The new King Grunt of roll-on power, the ZL1000 delivers a mid-range punch that crushes the V-Max and snuffs the FJ1200 dead in its tracks.' And in another, longer quote *Cycle* said:

With relatively short gearing and crisp responding curburation feeding on engine tuned to deliver neck-snaps on demand, the ZL1000's mid-range punch is a crushing force. The big Eliminator (the American market name for the model) leaves the ZL900 in its dust in the top three gears, blasting past Yamaha's FJ1200 and covering the zone 45 to 70 miles per hour [72 to 110km/h] in less time and distance than the almighty V-Max in fifth and sixth gears. For around town riding, the 'presence' of the big ZL engine, instantly responsive, full of silky strength, is power on an entirely different level from the original ZL900 Eliminator.

*TV star Patrick Mower (right) receiving the keys to his new LTD550 on 1 May 1981.*

But was the Eliminator, in either 900 or 1000 form, really a custom bike? If so, where were the high pulled-back bars? Or the front-mounted footrests and small 'peanut' fuel tank? And shouldn't a custom bike have kicked-out forks plus a soft power delivery? Instead, the ZL Eliminator series took its styling from the drag strips, hence the ultra-wide rear tyre (the 160/80–15 was the widest ever fitted onto a production bike at the time), skinny front, stepped bars, the conventional footrests and rake angle for the front forks, plus a massive 110bhp (on the 1000). Clearly this was intended as a performance machine, one with a kind of power capable of pushing the machine along very, very quickly indeed. It might not be a pure sports-bike in the accepted sense, but decent ground clearance, a conventional but very rigid steel chassis and a really tractable engine all conspired to make it a far better performer on twisty back roads than it ever had a right to be.

*The lightly customized SR650 was far less radical than the LTD range.*

*Using the engine from the newly released 1000RX liquid-cooled four, the ZL1000 Eliminator had 'roll-on' performance to equal anything on the road at its launch in 1987.*

A touring rider could also appreciate the ZL900/1000, too. For a start, the tank held around 20 litres (4.5 gal), and the shaft final drive was certainly a practical feature – as was the full rubber mounting of the power unit. The saddle was also wide and thickly padded and shaped for comfort. The ZL1000 motor was based around the 1000RX, as was the touring GTR. On the Eliminator, the sixteen-valve unit was similar to the GTR specification, but with the carb size increased by 2mm to 34mm, greater airbox capacity and an all-new exhaust system. The result was much improved over that of its touring-only brother, with tremendous mid-range stomp – snap open the throttle of the ZL1000 when cruising in top gear to notice just how superior it is to a GTR! As for looks, like most custom bikes you either loved or loathed it, but on the Eliminator series maybe even more so.

Although both the ZL900 and 1000 models sold well in the States, only the bigger model was imported into the UK, and it never sold in any quantity and was soon dropped. However, almost a decade later, in 1995, Kawasaki UK surprisingly decided to reimport the theme in the shape of the ZL600 Eliminator: in 1997 this sells for £5,725 and is the B variant of the earlier A model not being brought into Britain. The 592cc (60 x 52.4mm) liquid-cooled sixteen-valve motor is based on the company's ZZ-R600. Its specification includes four CVK30 carbs, valve-head diameters of 21.5mm inlet and 19mm exhaust, 11:1 compression cast-aluminium pistons running in reborable cast-iron liners pressed into an aluminium cylinder. The four exhaust pipes are made of double-wall steel which are bright chrome-plated, as are the two large-capacity mufflers. The clutch features a

*Although the ZL600 Eliminator had been on sale for several years across the Atlantic, British enthusiasts had to wait until 1995 before they could buy the drag strip-inspired model, powered by a four-cylinder liquid-cooled engine with shaft drive.*

'back-torque' limited system, which allows a small amount of clutch slippage to further reduce loads during extreme braking conditions.

There is a rubber-mounted, vertical flow, aluminium radiator with a single thermostat-controlled fan; six-speed transmission, shaft final drive and double cradle frame (with the downtubes passing *outside* the four exhaust pipes); it is long wheelbase (1,550mm/61in) and has a low seat height (715mm/28in) with wire wheels and 18/15in front/rear tyres. Braking is taken care of by an efficient 300mm semi-floating disc activated by a four-piston caliper at the front; rear stopping power is provided by a large 200mm SLS drum. The front forks have exposed, hard-chromed stanchions of 37mm (1.5in) diameter, whilst the twin rear shocks feature five-way preload. Dry weight is 200kg (441lb).

Kawasaki see the latest Eliminator as a modern machine which 'combines classic styling with custom dragster appeal'.

# 10 The GPZ900R

In its own way the GPZ900R was as equally important a machine for Kawasaki as was the original four-cylinder Z1, because if the legendary Z1 was the father of the air-cooled four-cylinder Kawasaki line, then the GPZ900R is without question the sire to the company's liquid-cooled family. The GPZ900R was shown to the world's press for the first time in December 1983, with production models coming on stream during early 1984. And what an impression it made on all who rode it, both press and public alike.

Known as the Ninja in North America, the 900R was the first Superbike with a liquid-cooled, sixteen-valve, dohc, in-line, four-cylinder engine. It was also the first to combine a lightweight diamond frame, aluminium rear frame section and 16in front wheel; and, Kawasaki claimed, the first with a front fork that delivered truly progressive wheel travel combined with the company's rising rate Uni-Trak rear suspension.

As with Z1, the centrepiece of the 900R was its engine. Here Kawasaki could look to the fact that this had been the main feature of every large displacement model for over a decade, and in that time a reputation had been cemented for *power with reliability*. However, realizing that time and technology would eventually catch up with the original Z-bike concept, the company began to test and retest every practical combination of chassis and powertrain to find the best suited to a second-generation Superbike. Although several other configurations showed promise, including a V4 and V6 and an in-line six, all were eventually judged to

*A GPZ900R being put under test at its world launch at Leguna Seca, late 1983. It was the first modern Superbike with a liquid-cooled, sixteen-valve dohc four-cylinder engine.*

offer no significant advantage over an across-the-frame four cylinder for sportsbike use. So the proven layout was retained, although virtually every other aspect was re-evaluated. The result was an all-new engine which took Kawasaki – and ultimately the rest of the Japanese industry – a giant step forwards.

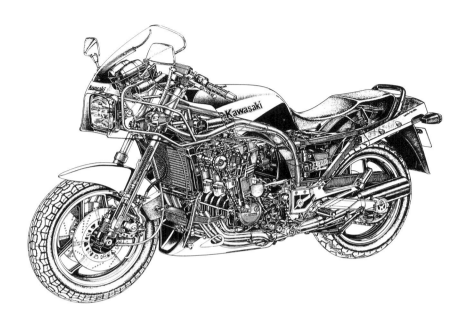

*Cutaway drawing
of the GPZ900R
showing its
technical features.*

*With a width of
just 541mm
(21.3in) the
GPZ900R engine
was a full 123mm
(4.84in) narrower
than the Z1
powerplant of a
decade earlier.*

Although the GPZ900R's included valve angle had been decreased more than 25 degrees (in comparison to both the 1983 GPz750 and 1100 models) to 34.9 degrees, the engine was shorter, top to bottom, than the original Z1, with a reduction of crank centre to the top of the cam cover of 24.5mm. The engine was also 48.26mm (1.9in) shorter front to back, and including the aluminium radiator, oil cooler, and all other engine components, was a full 5kg (11lb) lighter than that of the Z1. A major factor in this compact design was a basic change in the in-line four layout. Liquid cooling meant that the cam chain could be positioned outside the cylinder bank, giving the 900R a wet-liner cooling system that was both compact and highly efficient. This also allowed a more direct combustion path from gearbox to exhaust.

Revving to 10,500rpm, the one-piece crank was supported by five plain bearings which, in addition to driving the clutch, also drove a compact counterbalancer, which virtually eliminated secondary vibration.

At the business end of this sixteen-valve motor, a narrow valve angle (inlet 18.5 degrees and exhaust 16.4 degrees from vertical) allowed shorter ports for increased breathing ability and compact chambers for increased combustion efficiency. But despite the narrow included angle, Kawasaki's engineering team had been able to employ relatively large diameter valves (inlet 29mm, exhaust 24.7mm) which also contributed additional horsepower due to increased breathing efficiency.

With five bearings each, the two hollow lightweight camshafts turned in the head itself. Each cam had four lobes actuating two

*The 908cc (72.5 x 55mm) motor produced almost 114bhp and 8.7kg/m (62.93lb/ft) of torque.*

## Automatic Variable Damping System

With the advantage of hindsight, a couple of features on the GPz900R owed more to fashion than to pure function: one was the fitment of a 16in front wheel; the other what Kawasaki called AVDS (automatic variable damping system). In fact Kawasaki were able to claim a 'first on any Superbike' for AVDS, although just how much it really provided is open to question. The company's 1985 publicity blurb describes it in the following way:

> It provides truly progressive front suspension in two stages. Firstly, as the speed/distance of the front suspension travel increases, the main fork spring pushes down on the AVDS valve assembly to restrict hydraulic fluid transfer, and effectively increase compression damping. Then, as the compression force continues to increase, the valve is progressively forced open as the secondary AVDS spring compresses, assuring optimum performance under a wide variety of conditions. AVDS begins working after an average 50mm of suspension travel. Total travel is 140mm.

Besides its use on the GPZ900R, AVDS was also fitted to the GPZ750R, and the GPZ600R models.

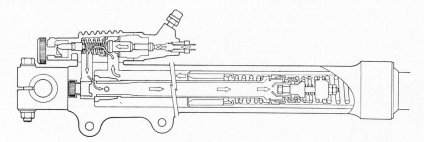

*Kawasaki's AVDS was claimed to deliver true progressive suspension in two stages. First, as the speed/distance of front suspension travel increased, the main fork spring pushed down on the AVDS valve assembly to restrict hydraulic fluid transfer, and effectively increased compression damping. Then, as compression force continued to increase, the valve was progressively forced open as the secondary AVDS spring compressed, assuring optimum performance. Well, that was the theory, anyway!*

*Feature of the original GPZ900R: automatic variable damping system and 16in front wheel.*

valves each through dual-finger cam followers. Valve adjustment was carried out by means of a screw and locknut. The cams themselves were driven by a Hy-Vo chain from the nearside of the crankshaft, and Kawasaki's newly introduced constant-load automatic tensioner ensured decreased mechanical loss and more consistent chain tension, while a 7.94mm chain pitch provided more strength than a conventional chain without any additional weight penalty.

The liquid-cooling system utilized a single aluminium cross-flow radiator, thermostat, electric fan and water pump. Water entered the cylinder liners at the front on the engine, flowed up and back through the head, then back to the radiator. The water pump was gear-driven off the clutch from the same shaft that drives the oil pump. Liquid cooling not only provided more scope for development in the future, but also additional benefits such as a decrease in piston/bore clearance and the ability to run a higher compression ratio.

The radiator held 0.731 litres (1.25 pints) and weighed 1.2kg (2.6lb). The thermostat opened at 87°C (188.6°F) and the fan actuated at 97°C (206.6°F) and continued to run even after the engine was switched off, to rid the system of any residual heat.

Lubrication was taken care of by a special dual-stage system. In the primary oil loop, lubricant was drawn through the primary filter to the pump, then passed through the filter element to the crank, gearbox head and other components. In the secondary loop, lubricant was passed from the pump to the four-tier oil cooler, then back to the wet sump.

The oil cooler served a secondary function as a temporary 'storage tank'. Sump oil level was therefore kept at a minimum, whilst a special dam isolated the critical area around the balancer gear, primary drive and clutch. This system resulted in a significant increase in mechanical efficiency. Lubrication was also given an extra boost since the cooler did not restrict oil flow to vital components. To help prevent leakage (maximum oil pressure 5kg/cm$^2$, 71.1psi), oil passed to and from the head via external lines.

Other important features of the power-plant included a large capacity airbox, maintenance-free ignition with electronic timing advancer, Keihan CVK34mm carbs and new silencers, with improved cornering

*The diamond frame was constructed in high-tensile steel tubing which Kawasaki claimed was stronger yet lighter than conventional steel tubing.*

clearance over previous four-cylinder Kawasakis.

As well as a new light-pull hydraulic clutch, the 900R featured a six-speed gearbox – a first for Kawasaki on a large bore machine. At 62.14mph (99.98km/h), the engine ran at a low 4,200rpm in top gear.

The gearbox shafts were staggered in the vertical plane to save space and reduce mechanical loss; there were undercut dogs for third, fourth and fifth gears, plus a positive neutral finder.

The GPZ900R's new, high-tensile steel frame cut about 5kg (11lb) off the weight of previous large capacity Kawasaki sports models; it also lowered the overall centre of gravity, allowing greater lean without sacrificing overall frame strength. In the early stages of frame testing, standard downtubes were added to determine what stress, if any, they would counter. But results showed that the downtubes carried virtually no load, so were subsequently removed.

There was a box-section, alloy swinging arm which employed eccentric cam drivechain adjusters. Supported inboard by the steel backbone frame and outboard by an alloy sub-frame, the needle-bearing swinging arm pivot synthetic bushes reduced side movement and contributed to the excellent handling qualities of the machine.

When Barry Hickmott tested one of the then new GPZ900Rs for *Motorcycle Enthusiast* back in 1984, he called the machine 'gentle giant', this coming from his surprise that the model 'would plod along at 1,000–1,200rpm without protest'. He went on to say:

Its ability remembering its 160mph [258km/h] top speed, to weave among the traffic was amazing. The crisp gear change and hydraulic clutch played their part, but it was the low seat height and 16in front wheel that allowed easy maneuvering and most important of all, safe stopping. If you think the GPZ900R is only suited to 6 foot muscle men then you are mistaken, I am just 5' 6", weigh 9 stone and suffer from ducks disease (short legs!), but I found the GPZ900R one of the easiest machines to persuade through, what turned out to be one of the biggest jams London has seen for ages.

*At the time of its debut the GPZ900R represented the cutting edge of big bike technology, with an unbeatable combination of speed, handling braking and rider comfort in a single package.*

But it was when he left the city that things really started to impress tester Hickmott:

> Moving north out of London and up the M1, I enjoyed my first real taste of the machine's open road performance. It shot up to 70mph [110km/h] with no effort whatsoever and registering just over 4,500rpm it was plainly obvious that 160mph [258km/h] was on tap at the tacho's 10,500rpm redline. However, the GPZ900R ambled along for mile after mile at the legal limit rock steady with no wind buffeting from the fairing and inspiring confidence as every minute past. Even from 4,500rpm the motor pulled away with arm-stretching acceleration and dropping a cog or two was totally unnecessary for overtaking – once in top it stayed there.

Back lanes provided just as much fun as motorways. Other points of the machine which brought praise were the brakes (twin 280mm discs front, single 270mm disc rear, all with dual piston calipers), powerful halogen headlamp, handlebar-mounted choke lever, comfortable deep foam seat – in fact Barry Hickmott only had one real complaint: Kawasaki wanted it back!

In standard form the 908cc (72.5 x 55mm) engine produced 114bhp and 8.7kh/m (62.93 ft/lb) of torque. Other technical details included automatic variable damping system (AVDS) anti-dive for the front forks, a stanchion diameter of 38mm (1mm up from the air-cooled 750/1100GPz models), six-spoke alloy wheels, V-rated tyres, 22l (4.75gal) fuel tank and a dry weight of 228kg (503lb).

*Motor Cycle News* achieved 158mph (254km/h) through their electronic test eye, whilst sales received a further boost when in June 1984 (just three months after its release onto the British market) a trio of GPZ900Rs showed the model's sporting potential when they filled the rostrum in the production TT. Headed by race winner Geoff Johnson, the Kawasaki trio (all dealer

*Milk Race duty for the GPZ900R in 1986.*

*Rider details included raised clip-on handlebars, hydraulic clutch, easy-to-read instruments, and handlebar-mounted choke control.*

*A GPZ900R being raced in the British production race series in 1984 by Ian Wilson, seen here at Donington Park.*

*1984 Production TT winner Geoff Johnson at Ramsey during his historic ride. All the first three machines in the 1300cc class were dealer-entered 900Rs.*

*1984 MCN Avon production TT class winners, Phil Mellor (left), Geoff Johnson (centre), and Trevor Nation celebrate in style.*

*Geoff Johnson and friends, with the TT winning machine at a show later that year.*

entered) finished ahead of all the works-supported teams from rival manufacturers. To round off a truly memorable year, readers of *Motor Cycle News* voted the 900R as their 'Machine of the Year'.

But the 900R wasn't perfect: early examples suffered a spate of warranty claims caused by faulty camshaft case-hardening and associated problems. However, these early glitches were easily overcome, and the GPZ900R was to prove one of the most durable, and longest running, of all the company's models. It was still being sold in the UK until as late as 1996. In that time there was only one real update, this coming in August 1989 with the launch of the A7 series.

Major changes were new forks with 41mm (1.6in) stanchions, new 300mm semi-floating front discs, new four-piston front calipers, new instrument panel, wider wheels (with a 17in front instead of the original 16in), adjustable brake and clutch levers, and new colours and graphics.

*There was also the smaller-engined GPZ750R shown here; it had less power and torque, but was the same weight, so performance was disappointing.*

115

In the early years (until it was replaced by the GPX750) there was also a GPZ750R. This was essentially the same as the 900R, but with 748cc (70 x 48.6mm) and 92bhp. Kawasaki claimed a top speed of 140mph (225km/h). In truth it was never a real success, living as it did in the shadow of its bigger, more powerful brother. It was also outpaced by rivals such as Suzuki's GSX-R750, Yamaha's FZ750 and Honda's VFR 750, and it was left for the GPX750 to redress the issue when it arrived in late 1986.

A fitting tribute to Kawasaki's ground-breaking GPZ900R would be to say that it achieved for its marque, in the 1980s, what the CBR900RR Fireblade did for

Honda in the 1990s. The final batch of 900Rs was imported and sold in the UK during 1996, making it one of the longest selling large capacity Japanese machines of all time.

In the eyes of the insurance industry the GPZ900R, nicknamed the 'King', became a Classic on 1 January 1998. A Classic is a motorcyle that has reached fourteen years of age. But as leading bike insurers Carol Nash Insurance Consultants Ltd said in their 1997 NEC Show *Cover Notes* magazine, 'This 908cc beauty, with its liquid-cooled, double overhead cam, inline four engine capable of whacking out 112bhp, has already secured its place in the annals of biking history. It's so distinctive compared to any other so-called plastics.'

*1990 GPZ900R. Improvements included: larger 41mm fork stanchions, 17in front wheel and semi-floating dual front disc brakes with four-piston calipers; AVDS was dropped.*

# 11 Liquid-Cooled Performance

## FIRST GENERATION LIQUID-COOLED 600: THE GPZ

In 1984 Kawasaki scored with the GPZ900R, and the following year, 1985, it did it again with the smaller GPZ600R – and in the process stole a march on the opposition by creating a whole new class, the liquid-cooled SuperSport 600. The 600R shared numerous features with its bigger brother, such as being an across-the-frame, four-cylinder four-stroke with double overhead camshafts and four valves per cylinder. However, it was far from being simply a scaled-down 900R, but was very much a new machine in its own right.

The engine, whilst having many similarities with the 900R, was actually more closely linked to the air-cooled GPz550's power-plant, which had proved surprisingly successful in production class racing on both sides of the Atlantic; in America it had proved particularly suitable in the box-stock category. Another asset was its exceptional reputation for reliability, with many professional race tuners considering the 550 unit to be one of the strongest ever built.

The liquid-cooled 592cc (60 × 52.4mm) continued this bullet-proof example. And it followed the 550's centre cam chain, chain primary drive with an intermediate shaft and crank-end alternator. The 600's engine was also more compact than the 550's – in fact it was a full 40mm narrower.

The five-bearing bottom end was virtually the same as the 550's. However, the bore centres of cylinders two and three had been moved inwards 1mm. The 600 had wet liners. Coolant entered each jacket through an inlet onto the back of the cylinders, flowed around the liners, passed through the head and exited via two outlets in the top. The single radiator was aluminium and was fitted with a thermostatically controlled electric fan. Except for cam-chain location, the head and valve train were similar to the 900R with valves actuated by cam followers carrying screw-type adjusters.

The all-new frame was manufactured primarily from rectangular section steel. Twin downtubes bolted to the main section near the steering head and swinging arm pivot, whilst three large cross-tubes in the main section ensured rigidity. An aluminium brace across the downtubes supported the radiator and oil cooler.

Sixteen-inch wheels ensured a low 770mm (30in) seat height, and an all-up weight of 195kg (430lb) certainly went a long way to making the bike controllable around town, whilst out on the open road a power output of 75bhp (10 more than the air-cooled GPz550) at 10,500rpm ensured brisk performance.

During its first two years, the 600R was easily the best selling machine in its class; but with the entry of the original Honda CBR 600 (coded F) in 1987, things changed: the Honda put out 83bhp and clocked 140mph

*After the GPZ900R (and its 750 brother), the next in the liquid-cooled GPZ family was the 600R; it shared numerous features with its bigger soulmates, such as dohc and four valves per cylinder.*

*However, the 600R chassis was no throwback to an earlier era. Instead, it was a double-triangulated perimeter frame of steel construction and mostly rectangular in construction.*

*Unlike the 750/900, the engine in the 600R simply 'sat' in its chassis, and used rubber engine mounts at the front – in the same fashion as the air-cooled 550.*

*The 592cc (60 x 52.4mm) engine, although having several similarities with the 750/900R, was actually based more closely on the air-cooled GPz550's unit.*

*Bank of four Keihin CVK 32mm carburettors.*

*Adam Woodhall (shown here) and Mike Potter shared this GPZ600R during the 1985 Snetterton Six-Hour Race. Overheating caused their eventual retirement.*

*Details of the automatic variable damping system (AVDS) anti-dive system on the 600R – basically identical to that used on the larger 750/900R models.*

*Yet another version of Kawasaki's Uni-Trak monoshock rear suspension.*

(225km/h) through the timing lights. From then on, the GPZ's days at the top were over.

## SECOND GENERATION LIQUID-COOLED 600: THE GPX

For 1988, Kawasaki introduced their new GPX600R. This second generation liquid-cooled 600 was armed with features from the GPX750R, and succeeded what had become the world's top selling middleweight sports bike, the GPZ600R. Modifications to the 600's powerplant had resulted in a 1.5kg (3.3lb) lighter, 13 per cent more powerful engine. Improved design to the inlet porting, new inlet valves, lighter pistons, chrome-molybdenum connecting rods, and a larger airbox were some of the major improvements. To match the increase in horsepower (85bhp at 11,000rpm), the radiator's cooling capacity was up by 23 per cent. Kawasaki claimed 143mph (230km/h) and the standing 400m (¼mile) in 11.6 seconds.

The GPX600R's frame was similar to the lightweight double cradle design on the GPX750. There were thus two major frame sections: a high-tensile steel main frame and a short, bolt-on box-section aluminium rear section. The 600's frame design differed only in the size and placement of gussets, brackets, and engine mounts.

Other new components were the fairing, the 38mm front forks sharing the same electric suspensions system introduced on the GPX750. The ESCS, or the electric suspension control system, combine the functions of automatic damping and anti-dive into one lightweight unit. ESCS valves opened and closed automatically according to the inner pressure of the fork to adjust compression damping in response to speed and distance of fork travel. For an instantaneous anti-dive effect, valves were electrically activated whenever the front brake was applied.

There were also new brakes – with BAC (balanced activation caliper) – and these were a feature not only on the larger GPX, but on the new ZX-10 Superbike, too.

Although 16in size wheels and tyres had been retained, careful engineering had seen the weight of the complete wheel assemblies (including hubs, brakes etc) cut by 3.5kg (7.7lb). The new V-rated Dunlop K205F tyres had been designed specially for the GPX and measured 110/80–V16 and 130/90-V16. The low aspect ratios of the tyres (80 per cent front and 60 per cent rear) helped to lower

*In 1987 the GPZ600 was joined by the GPX600. Modifications to the engine resulted in it not only being 1.5kg (3.3lb) lighter, but also 13 per cent more powerful.*

the seat height (755mm/30in), and also improved handling and provided more rider confidence.

A notable feature of the GPX600 was the fuel tap knob which was located on the left knee grip-pad.

The GPX600 proved a winner on the track too, winning many 600 SuperSport races during 1988. When the ZZ-R600 went on sale in 1990 everyone imagined that that would be the end of the road for the GPX600. But as with the GPZ600 which ran alongside the GPX, this is essentially what transpired – albeit with a blip when the machine wasn't imported into the UK during the early part of the 1990s. But in 1993 the GPX was re-introduced as a 'budget bike', Kawasaki's brochure reading 'Want a high performance middleweight but lack the necessary funds? Then look no further.' It was to remain on sale for another four years before finally being axed at the end of 1996, by which time the price had risen to £5,365.

## ZZ-R600

In October 1989 Kawasaki launched both the ZZ-R1100 and ZZ-R600. The latter was very much a machine which had both power and comfort. It was also a physically larger machine than both the GPZ and GPX models which preceded it; in fact the official factory information pack of the two stated: 'A grand touring motorcycle. It is upsized, and offers near the performance of a 750cc machine.' Its

*Kawasaki UK's racing arm Team Green campaigned the GPX600 in British SuperSport events; riders included Ray Swann, seen here at Oliver's Mount, Scarborough in September 1988.*

*By re-introducing the GPX600R to their 1993 range, Kawasaki UK were able to offer a sports middleweight with the budget price tag of £4,140 plus on-the-road charges.*

main competition was from Honda (CBR600) and Yamaha (FZR600).

The 599cc (64 x 46.6mm) was not an upstaged GPZ/GPX unit, but an entirely new design, although it was still dohc and sixteen-valve. The cylinder head featured straight-shot inlet ports with 26mm inlet and 22mm exhaust valves set at an efficient, compact 30-degree included angle. Added to this was an 11.5:1 compression ratio, 36mm Keihin CVKD carbs, digital ignition and a 4–1–2 exhaust system which had a special baffle to provide smooth power delivery across the rev range.

Like the engine, the frame was also new, with double box-section aluminium extrusions mated to a cast-alloy steering head, swinging arm pivot and downtube/side brace junction; Kawasaki claimed that the ZZ-R600 sported the stiffest frame ever fitted to one of their middleweights. At the rear, a high-tensile steel sub-frame, bolted on, supported the rider and provided mounting points for the battery, wiring and other detail items.

This was Kawasaki's first 600cc class machine to feature an aluminium mainframe, and linked to an engine producing almost 100bhp it was certainly a match for the opposing 600s, at least on the street. Its additional bulk was to limit its track success, however.

Beefy 41mm (1.6in) diameter front forks – the same size as those on the ZX-10 – helped to keep the front end in order. Braking also was uprated from the GPX, with new four-piston calipers mated to large 300mm floating discs up front, whilst a dual piston

*John Reynolds clinched the SuperSport 600 class of the British Supercup Championships for Team Green on his ZZ-R600 in 1990, the new bike's first production year. Model designation was ZX600D1.*

*The ZZ-R was Kawasaki's first 600-class machine to feature an aluminium mainframe. The engine was based on the GPX, but had been strengthened and given a power boost to almost 100bhp.*

caliper and 230mm rear disc provided the kind of braking feel that was once the preserve of litre-class machinery.

The new three-spoke cast alloy wheels featured large, hollow-hub castings to reduce weight. Tyres of 17in were now standard, and tyres measuring 120/60 and 160/60 being specified front and rear respectively.

But it was in the area of rider accommodation and comfort where the new Kawasaki really scored. With a large fairing, the ZZ-R offered good rider protection from the cold and rain, while at the same time allowing the machine to slip through the wind. There was also ample room on the extensive dual seat for both rider and passenger alike. It was in these areas that the ZZ-R really scored over its CBR and FZR rivals. Even so, like any bike, the ZZ-R600 was not without its faults – a snatchy transmission and infuriating 'fuel low' idiot lights which came on when the tank was only half empty, to name but two.

Realizing that even a good bike can be improved, Kawasaki engineers created a new version (together with an equally updated 1100 version) for 1993. This was announced in September 1992 as the EI (the 1990 model was coded DI). *Motor Cycle News* summed up the newcomer nicely in its 3 February 1993 test:

> Kawasaki's ZZ-R600 has been on a crash fitness course. The slightly soft-edged sports-tourer of 1992 has been transformed into a razor-sharp scratcher for '93. It's leaner, tauter, stronger – and much faster!

The changes which brought about this transformation included considerable work on the engine; lighter flywheel for quicker engine response; lighter pistons, pins and connecting rods to reduce reciprocating mass; smaller big-end pin size, lighter valve spring rates, lighter valve stems and cam followers, and shorter cylinder liners to reduce friction and boost power; also a twin-ram air-intake system to boost power (this

*For the 1993 season both the 1100 and 600 ZZ-R models were updated. This is one of the revised smaller bikes at the Birmingham NEC Show, late 1992. Factory coding designation was ZX600E1.*

*The 1993 model ZZ-R600E1 featured engine improvements, stronger frame, a more efficient fairing and better brakes.*

was adopted for the 1100 version as well).

Other changes included a stronger chassis with stiffer swinging arm; front brake discs skimmed by 0.5mm to reduce unsprung weight; a larger diameter (240mm) rear disc; a new fairing design with more efficient frontal area; handlebars moved back for shorter reach; and the instrument console area had been redesigned. Although the rake, trail and tyre profiles remained the same, 10mm (³/₈ in) had been lost off the wheelbase (down to 1,430mm/56in).

*Motor Cycle News* achieved a maximum speed (albeit with a strong tail wind!) of 163.4mph (262.9km/h) which they pointed out was more like 155mph (249km/h) under neutral conditions. This was still good, compared with other *MCN* figures: Honda NR750 (hi-tech oval piston 157mph/253km/h), Triumph 1200 Daytona (160mph/257km/h), Ducati 851 (151mph/243km/h) and Suzuki GSX-R750 (154mph/248km/h). As for the 600s its main rival, the Honda CBR (151mph/243km/h) was beaten, hands down.

Although weight had been lost off the frame and brake discs, it had been put on elsewhere, and the 1993 ZZ-R600 weighed in at the same 195kg (430lb) as the model it replaced. *MCN* summed it up:

The ZZ-R600 is an excellent all-round bike. Although sportier than the previous model, it is still extremely comfortable, has excellent weather protection and performs brilliantly. It is actually difficult to fault – the brakes are the only weakness, and I found the front end sensitive to side winds. After that, it is down to taste!

There is no doubt that the ZZ-R600 is more of a tourer than the narrower-focus Honda and Yamaha models; this also means it never had the amount of exposure in 600

SuperSport racing events. It is still in production and selling steadily, even though Kawasaki now has its own narrow focus ZX-6R sportster.

## GPX750

It may come as a surprise, but when the GPX750R was launched in September 1986, it was the first Kawasaki four-cylinder model designed exclusively as a 750. Based on the technology already well proven in previous Kawasaki engines, the GPX powerplant was radically lighter and narrower than the company's previous 750, and claimed by Kawasaki to be the most compact 750 four available. Contributing factors included an all-new valve train similar to that introduced the previous year in the twin-cylinder GPZ250R; minimum mass components throughout, including pistons weighing just 165g (6oz) each; a compact new primary drive and gearbox design; and a belt-driven alternator behind the cylinders. The result was a 750 which put out 106bhp at 10,500rpm and 7.8kg/m of torque at 8,500rpm.

Powered by a liquid-cooled, sixteen-valve, dohc motor, the GPX750 displaced 748cc (68 x 51.5mm) and ran on a compression ratio of 11.2:1 with maintenance-free, electronic ignition and four Keihan CVK 34mm carbs. With a dry weight of 195kg (430lb) it was the second lightest machine in its class when launched.

The GPX also marked the high-level water mark for the Japanese industry's 1980s love of smart abbreviations for its latest technical gizmos – there were no less than six: RPMS (redline plus maximum mass-reduction system), HI-TECH (High-velocity induction technology), DADS (dry alternator drive system), FAST frame (featherweight Aluminium and steel technology frame),

*When the GPX750R was launched in September 1986, it was the first Kawasaki four to be designed exclusively as a 750. This is one of the initial production batch.*

*GPX750R cylinder head specially cut away to show the all-new valve train similar to that introduced the previous year in the twin-cylinder GPZ250R.*

ESCS (electric suspension control system) and BAC (balanced actuation calipers). But just in case you are overawed, or more likely totally overwhelmed by this mass of technical speak, the GPX750R was actually a rather nice motorcycle.

When *What Bike?* tested an F3 variant in their July 1989 issue, tester Brian Crichton was highly impressed, giving the top five-star marking to the sections on *Engine and Transmission'*, *'Chassis'*, *'The Price you pay'*, and *'Conclusion'*. In the latter he said:

> A masterpiece of miniaturization, the GPX750R is like a Fabergé egg: full of treats, all of them better than you would ever have expected. It's not without its faults: and style wise, though smart, it doesn't stand out from the crowd. Beyond these considerations it's a dance with delight.

With a maximum speed of 151mph (243km/h), it was only a mere 1mph (1.6km/h) slower than the bike which replaced it in Kawasaki line, the ZXR750. And although the GPX looked positively dated against the new ZXR, it was actually a much superior *streetbike*. For example, the GPX's specification included a comfortable pillion seat, centre and side stands, exceptionally good suspension, and fully usable rear view mirrors – ball and socket, they could be adjusted exactly where you wanted them. Retractable luggage locks were fitted so that luggage could be strapped across the seat. There was also a hand recess to help when pulling the machine onto the mainstand, plus a passenger grab rail and two helmet locks. New for the 1989 specification model was the heating of the inlet manifold, to prevent carburettor 'icing' which had proved something of a Kawasaki gremlin, not just on the GPX750, but on several other models of the same era, including the

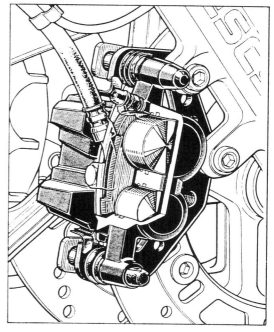

The GPX750 was the first Kawasaki to employ the BAC (balanced actuation caliper) system. These were dual-piston calipers with a difference, where the leading piston had a smaller diameter than the trailing pistons.

GPZ900R. This got so bad at one stage that Kawasaki had to mount a recall programme to cure it once and for all. On the 1989 GPX750, water ducting to the inlet was employed, which effectively solved the problem.

No bike is perfect, and certainly not the GPX with an annoying hesitation between 3,000 and 4,000rpm as probably the worst offender. Other minus points were collected by the use of 16in front and 18in rear wheels; a fairing which did no favours for the pillion passenger (who, unlike the rider, suffered from unwanted buffeting about the head at high speeds); and a woefully weak horn. The machine's main forte was its 'all-rounder'

## GPX750 Technical Gizmos

### RPMS (Redline Plus Maximum Mass-Reduction System)
In the GPX's valve train, two short, hollow camshafts actuated sixteen valves through individual lobes and rocker arms. As in the system introduced on the GPZ250R the previous year, individual rockers reduced reciprocating mass and eliminated the chance of uneven cam lobe loading. Lash adjusters were on the pivot end of each rocker, further reducing reciprocating mass. And the rockers pivoted on rods, which were anchored at the sides of the head instead of in the middle; this allowed Kawasaki's engineering team maximum freedom in port design, and the GPX's smoothly curved, tapered ports benefited in the increased breathing efficiency. Specific RPMS benefits included reduced bulk, an included valve angle of only 30 degrees, and the capacity to rev the valve train to 14,500rpm in stock form (although maximum engine revs – stock – were 11,500rpm).

### HI-TECH (High-Velocity Induction Technology)
The new power-boosting induction system improved breathing efficiency in two steps: first, special ducts with patented 'ramp vents' smoothed the air flow into the semi-flat-slide carbs for a non-turbulent, high-speed stream of air. Second, this high-velocity charge was carried to the cylinders through intake ports that tapered smoothly for maximum efficiency.

### DADS (Dry Alternator Drive System)
In this exclusive charging system, the alternator was driven by a multi-V belt, which was lighter than a chain and eliminated the need for a damper. DADS was easier to service or modify, and the alternator could be removed easily for racing.

### FAST Frame (Featherweight Aluminium and Steel Technology Frame)
Unlike many designs, the FAST frame was not based on alloy construction. It is a fact that aluminium is not only expensive, it is also more difficult to weld, repair or modify than a steel structure. So using modern CAE-CAD techniques, Kawasaki settled upon a high-tensile steel mainframe and a short alloy rear section, which actually weighed *less* than the competition all-alloy structures. This was a major reason for the machine's overall low dry weight.

### ESCS (Electric Suspension Control System)
The 38mm braced fork featured Kawasaki's first electric suspension system, which combined the functions of AVDS (as used on the GPZ750/900R) and anti-dive in one lightweight assembly. ESCS valves opened and closed automatically according to the inner oil pressure of the fork, to adjust compression damping according to the speed and distance of fork travel. In addition the unit was activated electrically whenever the front brakes were applied for instantaneous anti-dive effect.

### BAC (Balanced Actuation Calipers)
These dual-piston calipers, claimed Kawasaki, outperformed existing single- and dual-piston streetbike calipers. If dual pistons are the same diameter, more force is exerted at the leading edge of the long brake pad due to natural friction, negating the potential advantage of a dual-piston set-up. With Kawasaki's BAC, however, the pistons were of different diameters, to balance the braking force and spread this more evenly across the pad for less grab, improved feel and longer service life.

*A 1989 GPX750R F3 model: except for new colours/graphics, and heating of the inlet manifold (common on car engines) to prevent carburettor 'icing', it was the same specification as the original model.*

*In 1987 Kawasaki UK entered a team of three GPX750s in the Isle of Man TT. Riders left to right: Grant Gooding, Mac McDiarmid and Howard Selby.*

ability; it was just as happy carrying two people as one, unlike more single-purpose models such as the GSX-R750, the RC30 and its replacement, the ZXR750. Even so, it was able to give a good account of itself on a race track, as witnessed by a team of GPX750s competing successfully in the Isle of Man TT during 1987.

The British press launch took place at Castle Combe race circuit where a number of journalists put the GPX750R through its paces. John Robinson (technical editor of *Performance Bikes* and probably the most experienced tester amongst those present) commented:

> The GPX was the first bike I have actually enjoyed riding around Castle Combe! The circuit is so bumpy that the front wheel can be lifted clear off the ground when you are cranked over. The Kawasaki's suspension was very impressive: I was amazed at the way in which it coped with the surface at high speed. Most machines do not provide sufficient suspension adjustment, but with the GPX, every setting made a discernable difference. The handling itself proved extremely stable, yet it is very fast-responding when directional changes are required.

Racer and freelance journalist Steve Bateman, who had raced at Castle Combe several times on his own Formula 1 Harris-framed Suzuki GSX-R750, was also there, and recorded consistent times of 1 min 11 secs – fisec better than the existing 750cc production lap record, which at that time was held by Dave Hill on a Suzuki GSX-R750. Steve Bateman was particularly impressed with the ground clearance (which says a lot considering the centre stand was still in place!) and that the motor had got 'more torque than a GSX-R'.

Three days after the press had their first taste of the GPX750R at Castle Combe, *Performance Bikes* staffman Rupert Paul entered one of the machines in the world record weekend at Elvington, north Yorkshire. At the end of the meeting he was the new British national record holder of both the flying start quarter mile (145.86mph/234.69km/h) and the flying start kilometre (145.72mph/234.46km/h). These speeds were set from the average of runs made in each direction; and the best *one way* speed was a recorded 149mph (239.7km/h). The machine was absolutely standard with original road gearing and stock tyres.

## THE ZX NINJA FAMILY

The ZX Ninja family has been released onto the market in stages. First for 1994 came the ZX-9R, then in 1995 the ZX-6R and finally the ZX-7R went on sale in 1996. The '900' is a magical number for Kawasaki as it sired machines which have redefined motorcycling history, such as the Z1 and GPZ900R. It had been twenty years since the former and ten years since the latter appeared and Kawasaki fully expected the new ZX-9R Ninja to be just

*Top-of-the-range ZX-9R, Kawasaki's challenger to the class-leading Honda Fireblade in the 900cc stakes, arrived at the end of 1993, for the 1994 model year.*

## ZXR750 Development and Racing History

At the end of 1982, Kawasaki announced the withdrawal of their factory road-racing teams – a shock announcement at the time, for the company had won no less than eight 250cc and 350cc world championship titles in the previous five years, and their innovative monoque chassis 500cc racer was showing real promise. However, the ever-widening gap in technology between two-stroke race bikes and four-stroke roadsters meant that the vast cost of racing was hard to justify.

But . . . racing is hard to resist, and the factory had long been involved in endurance racing, mainly via Team Kawasaki France who have such an impressive record in this specialist sport. In 1985 they prepared a GPZ750R for this class, although it soon became evident that a sleeved-down 900 was not the way forward.

With the introduction of the GPX750R in 1987, the factory had a new machine on which they could base their endurance race programme. At the same time, however, Kawasaki was able to build a new chassis with a race-kitted GPX750 engine for works rider Kork Ballington to race at the Japanese Suzuka Eight-Hour race, where the machine conformed to Formula 1 rules which permitted one-off frames. This machine was designated the ZXR-7. The hand-crafted

*In late 1989 Kawasaki launched its first ZXR750 (coded H1) at the Estoril circuit in Portugal.*

perimeter-style chassis was constructed from sheet aluminium folded to shape and then welded top and bottom, which not only resulted in a very rigid structure, but enabled just the required amount of strength to be designed in at each point to minimize weight. Very labour-intensive to build, only a few were ever made – which probably explains why the British importers were somewhat upset when Roger Hurst, riding for Team Green UK, dropped the ZXR-7 he had been loaned for the Isle of Man in 1988. Actually that machine was repaired, but Roger then wrote it off a few weeks later at Thruxton!

In late 1989 Kawasaki launched its first ZXR750 – the H1 model – at Estoril in Portugal: although clearly a further development of the GPX750 roadster, it also included a wealth of experience gleaned from the Formula 1 and endurance racing programme. Replacing the GPX's conventional steel-tube frame was an all-aluminium perimeter component, though made from box-section extrusions rather than sheet, welded to aluminium castings at

*An unusual underside shot of a ZXR750H1, showing the linked exhaust, Uni-Trak and centre stand details.*

*A 1990 ZXR750, with uprated engine and new works F1-type swinging arm.*

the steering head and swinging arm pivot. Race-track practice was clearly evident in the distinctively braced, box-section aluminium swinging arm with a bolt on bracket at the rear to speed chain replacement, plus features such as built-in provisions for fitting a race-stand and steering damper.

Like the works F1 racer, conventional wide-diameter, cartridge-style fork stanchions were employed, while the front brakes featured semi-floating discs with four-piston calipers – a first for Kawasaki. Yet more track influence was revealed by the use of bottom-link Uni-Trak rear suspension which now featured an eccentric cam in its linkage to alter the ride height settings. The 17in wheels were ready to take racing tyres too, featuring extra wide rims and large hollow hubs and spokes to minimize unsprung weight.

Visually the ZXR750 looked every inch a race bike, too, a feeling heightened by the dramatic twin 'Hoover' tubes which ran from the front on the fairing to the fuel tank. This led to lots of speculation at first, though in reality they were merely ducting extra-cool air onto the cylinder head. The engine itself was extensively up-rated from the GPX 750, with an all-new top end giving better breathing, a higher compression ratio, bigger 36mm carbs, digital ignition and a 4-2-1 exhaust system.

For those interested in racing in either F1 or the then fledgling Superbike class, an engine race kit was made available, while the factory limited their activities to the ZXR-7, which finished runner up at the Le Mans Twenty-Four-Hour race that year.

In 1990, the production bike incorporated most of the engine parts from the previous season's race kit. At the same time, a new cylinder head with larger ports was fitted, together with bigger carbs, larger capacity curved radiator and new 4-into-1 exhaust. A useful amount of weight – 5kg(11lb) – was shaved from the chassis, while the braced swinging arm was ditched in favour of a stiffer, neater item based on the factory's latest F1 racer. More track influence was seen in the front suspension which gained both spring preload and damping adjustment, and the rear wheel rim grew still wider.

In that same year, 1990, Kawasaki was placed second and third at the famous Bol d'Or round of the FIM World Endurance Championship with factory ZXR-7s; but it was the ZXR750 that really began to attract attention by the successes it was notching up world-wide. In WSB (World Super Bike) racing, Rob Phillis riding for Team Kawasaki Australia was always amongst the leaders, and eventually finished fourth overall after numerous top five finishes, including wins in Australia and New Zealand. Riding for Team Muzzy, Doug Chandler contested just two WSB rounds and really upset the form book: first he won the prestigious American round overall to give Kawasaki their first ever World Super Bike victory; and then he repeated this success in Japan. In fact Doug's real task that year was to contest the AMA (American Motorcycle Association) Superbike Championship – and he secured victory after only seven of the eight-round series. This followed four outright wins, a second and a third.

By now Superbike racing had really captured the hearts and imagination of sponsors, spectators and television – and the manufacturers – so in 1991 Kawasaki launched not one, but a pair of 750-class SuperSports models. The new ZXR750 (J series) was aimed squarely at the road-going enthusiast, whereas the ZXR750R (K series), though fully street-legal, had a more track-biased specification, with a comprehensive race kit available to turn it into a very competitive racer. By using this twin-bike approach, Kawasaki could provide the streetbike rider with a practical sports machine, or the race rider with a 'racer-for-the-road' at very competitive prices, rather than a very expensive, limited-run machine designed purely for racing.

It was easy to see the original F1 factory racer influence on these 'new generation' models, from the highly efficient air management systems of the bodywork through to the perimeter frames. The latter comprised rails made from sheet-aluminium pressings welded top and bottom, which in turn were welded to large, hollow-section aluminium castings at the steering head and swinging arm pivots. Using the engine as a stressed member, the resulting frame provided extreme stiffness with the minimum of weight – a full 4kg (8.8lb) lighter than its predecessor. A bolt-on rear section made of square-section aluminium tubing was also featured.

*A 1993 ZXR750R: ram air induction – just like the works superbike racers – plus extra chassis rigidity.*

The swinging arm also adopted the works-racer, welded sheet-aluminium-style construction, while use of upside-down front forks complemented the frame's extra rigidity; these were of the cartridge type with 43mm stanchions (41mm on the ZXR-750R).

Not only was the engine redesigned to allow the camshaft to be driven from the offside end of the crankshaft rather than the centre, but by opting for a shorter stroke design – changed from the original 68 x 51.5mm to 71 x 47.3mm) – it allowed higher revs, the wider bore bringing the benefits of increased combustion and breathing efficiency.

Though in different states of tune, both new bikes shared an all-new cylinder head, valve train, pistons, crank and oil system. The camshaft drive redesign incorporated a lightweight individual rocker train, and all this allowed Kawasaki's design team to opt for an amazingly compact 20-degree included valve angle. There was a larger 8.7-litre (1.8 gal) airbox and a less restrictive 4-into-1 exhaust. Technical differences between the two engines that altered power characteristics included carburettors, cam timing, cam duration and compression ratios.

Other changes included larger 320mm (previously 310mm) semi-floating discs at the front, and wider rims and tyres, plus F1 works pattern bodywork – the J roadster having a dual stepped seat, the K ('R') version a solo type. The K model also featured revised cam profiles, flat-slide carburettors, close-ratio transmission, uprated suspension and an alloy fuel tank.

On the WSB scene the revised bike made an instant impact: by the end of 1991, Aussie Rob Phillis was the highest placed non-Ducati rider in the series, with third place in the championship. And in the FIM world endurance series, Team Kawasaki France started the season on ZXR-7 factory specials, but for the prestigious Bol d'Or switched to ZXR750R-based machines and took first and third places. They stayed with their bikes, and the result was a blistering one–two in the final championship table at season's end.

*John Reynolds became a double British champion in 1992, winning both the national and Supercup titles.*

In the USA, Scott Russell won the AMA 750cc SuperSport series with a perfect score of nine wins from nine races! Further north, in Canada, Steve Crevier won both the National 750cc Production Championship, and the Canadian Superbike Championship; while 'down under' Aaron Slight won both the Pan Pacific Superbike Championship and the Australian Superbike titles. In the all-important Japanese TT Formula 1 championships, Takahiro Sohwa scooped three rounds outright, and Michael Dowson of Australia another.

*Virtually no one was able to beat Reynolds in 1992; here he lifts the front wheel of his factory-backed ZXR750 after another convincing victory.*

For the 1992 model year, the ZXR750 was virtually unchanged except for colours and graphics – although significantly the race kit included a forerunner of ram-air induction, ducting air from below the steering head to the airbox, and the race wins simply kept on coming. Scott Russell took victory in the Daytona 200-miler in the then fastest-ever time, before going on to win the AMA Superbike Championship; but the by-now veteran racer Rob Phillis once again had to be content with third place in the WSB, still the quickest of the four-cylinder machinery. Team Kawasaki France notched up their second successive victory in world endurance, while Britain's John Reynolds totally dominated 750cc racing, winning both the TT Superbike and televized Supercup championships, backed by team-mate Brian Morrison. On their home territory, Kawasaki scooped both first and second places in the All-Japan TT-F1 event with Tsukamoto and Kitagawa.

The growing importance of Superbike racing world-wide meant that the pressure was on Kawasaki's engineers to continue the pace of their development in the 750cc sector – and this was to result in the ZXR750 L and M series, launched on 30 September 1992.

### Further Successes

For the third time in succession the Japanese factory won the world endurance crown, with the added satisfaction of winning on home ground at Suzaka; this was also the very first time the eight-hour event had been collected by Kawasaki. The riders who created this piece of history were Australian Aaron Slight and American Scott Russell. Taking the All-Japan TT-F1 event for the second consecutive year was the additional icing on the cake! Scott Russell's second Daytona 200 victory came in early March 1994, but in the fiercely contested WSB championship he had to relinquish his treasured No. 1 place, though its fate was never certain until Britain's Carl Fogarty ran out the champion at the very last round, riding a Ducati V-twin.

After the ZXR750 had turned in so many major championship victories world-wide since its conception five years earlier, the 1995 race season was one of mixed results. The season started well enough with Scott Russell again winning at Daytona, but his departure to 500cc grand prix racing deprived Kawasaki of the chance of world Superbike success, though Jockhim Schmidt won the important German Pro Superies series. Also second Team Muzzy rider, the young Australian Anthony Gobert, convincingly demonstrated that the ZXR still had the ability to win races at world championship level; indeed, he won the very last race of the 1995 series – but it was clear at this point that the opposition were catching up, and that the ZXR750 needed a worthy successor.

And that was to signal the entry of the Ninja ZX-7R.

*1992 Team Green British Championship pairing of John Reynolds (3) and Brian Morrison (6).*

as ground-breaking . . . but they were to be disappointed. Instead of being at the very cutting edge, the actual machine turned out to be more a mix of the ZZ-R1100 and ZXR750 already in production.

The 899cc (73 x 53.7mm) displacement was largely achieved by starting with the existing ZXR750 which was bored and stroked to provide the extra capacity but with a lower bore/stroke ratio. Kawasaki engineers real-ized that combustion had to be improved so it was a case of a major head redesign *and* an increase in bore size.

They retained the same valve sizes and cam timing as the ZXR750L1 and K1 (which effectively detuned the motor in 899cc form) and did a fair amount of work around the combustion chamber. The pistons featured a slightly dished crown and there was a narrow, 20-degree included angle between the valves; the reason for this was to get a combustion chamber that was compact, which isn't always as straightforward as it sounds. The pentroof shape of the cylinder head and the clearance to the piston depends on the angle between the inlet and exhaust valves, and this depends on the spacing between the cams, which in turn depends upon the size of the drive sprockets, which must be twice as large as the sprocket on the crankshaft. If the sprocket is carried between crank throws then it has to be larger than the diameter of the crankshaft and this severely limits cylinder head design. So the cam drive usually appears on the end of the crankshaft, where the smallest sprocket size is dictated by maximum engine speed. Even so, finger rockers were also employed to increase the spacing between the cams and provide an even narrower valve angle.

Despite all this effort, it appeared Kawasaki still had a combustion problem with the ZX-9: precisely their use of 10mm twin ground-electrode spark plugs and an ignition advance of 45 degrees above 5,800rpm. In comparison the earlier ZXR750J had 42.5 degrees at 6,200rpm and its combustion was fairly borderline. At the same time, the Kawasaki's engineering team provided larger 40mm CV carbs (the same as the ZZ-R1100). There was also a 12-litre (2fl gal) airbox, with two larger intake vents than the ZXR750 models and a pair of deep resonator boxes near each one to take out induction noise. The exhaust looked like a four into one but had separate pipes one and two for three and four, effectively making it a 4-2-1 system.

All in all, the ZX-9R engine appeared to have been developed with mid-range as much a priority as maximum speed – very much like the ZXR750, in fact.

The transmission also followed ZXR pattern, with the 'back-torque limiter' in the clutch (which makes the clutch slip slightly when it is transmitting reverse torque, reducing the chances of rear wheel hop during braking) and the same ratios in the six-speed box. What the engineering team did change, however, was the primary reduction ratio which was raised by almost 15 per cent. This achieved several things: it raised the overall gearing to match the increased torque of the bigger engine; it lowered the tooth loading on the individual gears; and it added 15 per cent to the inertia of the clutch and input shaft. This may have helped gearbox reliability, but it meant the gears were spinning faster and were therefore harder to shift.

Another problem which can happen when engines are uprated – in size or power – is that their vibration characteristics change, and the more power they give, the rougher they tend to run. This meant that even with part-rubber mountings, the ZX-9R had a rough patch which unfortunately coincided with top gear road-cruising speeds and manifests itself with vibes through the handlebars and footrests.

Weight was another problem. This had steadily increased, from the competitive 195kg (430lb) of the ZXR750J1, the L/M models being a few kg heavier, through to the ZX-9R at an extra 20kg – that is 215kg (474lb). This meant the balance was changed from being neutral or slightly tail-heavy to nose-heavy.

The steering geometry was also changed – a longer wheelbase, but steeper castor and less trail than the ZXR750 L/M models.

The forks remained at 41mm (they were reduced from 43mm on the ZXR750 J/K models in order to save weight) and front and rear suspension were given bump and rebound damping adjustment like the 750R variant.

The spring 1996 issue of *What Bike?* really summed up the pros and cons of the original ZX-9R:

## 1998 Ninja ZX-9R

Only the name and tyre sizes stay the same: the engine, frame, swing arm, wheels, brakes, exhaust, instruments and bodywork are all new. There's more power – and a lot less weight (down a massive 35kg to 183kg dry!). More handling and braking – and a lot less of everything else, except comfort and stability.

Every aspect of its predecessor has been re-examined and made smaller/lighter/better. Nett result is litre-style performance with the feel of a 600.

### Engine
- Bigger bore/shorter stroke allows bigger valves and reduces piston speed
- More compact with weight-saving, World Super Bike-style, magnesium covers for head, clutch, generator, igniter and chain
- Direct valve actuation for more precision
- Extra-small alternator moved from behind cylinders to end of crankshaft
- Lighter crankshaft for greater throttle response
- Liquid-cooled oil cooler
- K-TRIC (*Kawasaki Throttle Responsive Ignition Control*) – a throttle position sensor linked to ignition system for optimum timing at all throttle settings
- Titanium muffler.

### Chassis
- More compact frame has Ninja-style pressed sheet aluminium construction, but without the front downtubes and with new extruded aluminium swing arm
- Lighter and with 25mm shorter wheelbase for more responsive handling
- New, fully adjustable, conventional front forks with 46mm dia. stanchions
- New piggy-back rear shock with more adjustability
- Lighter front disc brakes with 6-piston calipers
- Lighter, hollow spoke, wheels.

### Bodywork
- All new styling is ultra 'clean' – the advanced aerodynamics and level of detailing – emphasizing its compact size, and ergonomically precise riding position
- Flush-fitting multi-reflector headlamp, all-new tail light with slim race-type seat cowl
- LCD displays for odometer, trip meter and clock.

*The new-for-1998 ZX-9R is at last the machine Kawasaki always hoped it would be, and fully capable of matching the class-leading Honda Fireblade.*

Kawasaki's attempt to outdo the Fireblade, the ZX-9's too heavy and too softly suspended to beat it in the bends. It's more comfy, though, and the engine's close to ZZ-R1100 levels of performance. The front brakes are eyeball-popping, but as a package the Blade is better.

Next in the revolution of the ZX family came the ZX-6R a year later for 1995. To be honest, although maybe it didn't push Honda's CBR off top spot, it at least equalled the class leader, and in some areas actually beat it.

*New for 1995, the ZX-6R F1 at the NEC Show in Birmingham, November 1994.*

Starting with the engine, the design team virtually threw away its blueprints for what had gone before in the Kawasaki liquid-cooled 600 pack (GPZ, GPX and ZZ-R). The engineering squad's first task was to create a lighter, more compact powerplant. To achieve this, the new engine was given a cam chain relocation from the centre to the offside end of the crankshaft; this meant a crank 30mm narrower than before. This also had the advantage of reducing width whilst maintaining crankshaft strength and also only five main journals were needed to support the crank (one less than on the ZZ-R), reducing weight, friction and mechanical loss.

A new engine/transmission meant the crankshaft-to-driveshaft distance decreased by 15mm to 133mm, whilst the driveshaft-to-driven shaft decreased 7mm to 58mm.

There were totally new bore and stroke measurements of 66 x 43.8mm (ZZ-R 64 x 46.6mm), giving 599cc. The short stroke and shortened connecting rod length reduced engine height from the crank to the cylinder head by 4mm. There was a pentroof combustion chamber design and 11.8:1 compression ratio (12:1 ZZ-R) offering higher combustion efficiency from the larger bore.

Reducing the included valve angle from 30 to 25 degrees allowed the use of larger valves: inlet 26 to 27mm, exhaust 22 to 22.6mm, for improved breathing.

The cylinder block was canted forwards 28 degrees (13 degrees more than ZZ-R) for reduced engine height. Two additional benefits of this move were first, a more downdraught position of the carbs for the mixture into the inlet ports, and second, a lower centre of gravity.

There was also a host of other, smaller engineering changes, many of which were expressly aimed at further reducing friction and mechanical loss; for example, the journal diameter of the crankshaft was reduced from 32 to 30mm for exactly this reason.

*ZX-6R Ninja engine assembly.*

Also, much attention was given to providing a smoother, more positive gearbox action. The transmission gear shift on the ZX-6R incorporated smaller involute splines for reduced drivetrain lash; gear width increased and there were now five dogs instead of six for second through to sixth gears, and they were undercut. Finally, shift fork rigidity had been increased.

To cope with the extra power, new coolant passages routing coolant around the exhaust port area were introduced to help maintain consistent operating temperature under hard road riding or racing usage.

The ZX-6R's mainframe, subframe and swinging arm were all manufactured in aluminium.

Conventional 41mm cartridge front forks featured twelve-way rebound damping, eleven-way compression damping and initial spring preload adjustability.

At the rear, Kawasaki's familiar bottom link Uni-Trak system had been given a nitrogen-charged shock with internal bladder reservoir featuring four-way rebound damping, nineteen-way compression damping and threaded collar, spring preload adjuster.

Attention to detail continued, with hollow, 20mm front and rear wheel spindles and hollow swinging arm pivot.

Semi-floating, radially drilled 300mm stainless steel front discs and four-pot calipers took care of the braking at the front, whilst a single 230mm disc steadied things up at the other end.

Hollow, three-spoke, cast-aluminium 17in wheels carried 120/60 ZR (front) and 160/60 ZR (rear) tyres.

Although new, the fairing was very similar to that found on the larger ZX-9R, making the two machines virtually identical visually.

In performance testing by the American magazine *Motorcyclist* and the British *Motor Cycle News* in December 1994, the ZX-6R achieved a maximum speed of 156mph (251km/h) whilst the standing 400m (¼ mile) was despatched in 11 seconds at a speed of 124.5mph (200km/h). As a comparison, Honda's CBR600 achieved 156mph (251km/h), 11.2secs and 122mph (196km/h); Yamaha's FZR600 141mph (227km/h), 11.7secs and 119mph (191km/h); and Suzuki's RF600 143mph (230km/h), 11.6secs and 116mph (187km/h). The tester quickly realized it was a two-horse race and summed it up:

This is a tough one. The Kawasaki offers raw power and glory, the Honda is a subtle blend of power and handling. Both are incredibly fast with the ZX-6R scoring extra points for advancing the class with its alloy frame and amazing engine (97.7bhp at 12,600rpm against

## 1998 Ninja ZX-6R

For 1998 the ZX-6R gains a new short-wheelbase aluminium frame with revised steering geometry, offering improvement in handling for both the street and race circuit. The engine also receives attention, gaining new carbs with Kawasaki Throttle Responsive Control (K-TRIC) which smoothes out the power characteristics.

### Engine
- Liquid-cooled, 16-valve dohc 599cc engine is more compact, lighter in weight and quicker
- New BDSR36R semi-downdraught carbs with K-TRIC improve power characteristics and throttle response across the range
- Crankshaft design improved with larger diameter ACG taper and strengthened crank-pins for greater reliability
- Exhaust manifold and pipes made almost entirely from stainless steel
- New ACG uses rare-earth magnets for high output, low weight and reduced engine width for deeper lean angles
- Improved piston materials
- Refinements to cam drive and primary gears have significantly reduced mechanical noise. The H version, available in certain markets, features the KLEEN catalyser system.

### Frame
- Shorter wheelbase, all-aluminium frame.

### Suspension
- New 46mm cartridge front fork. Features 12-way rebound damping, 10-way compression damping and initial spring preload adjustability

### Brakes
- Smaller diameter 5mm thick rear brake disk measures 220mm in diameter to reduce unsprung weight.

### Wheels and Tyres
- New rear wheel features wider 5.5in rim.

### Bodywork
- Windscreen is 15mm higher from improved wind protection
- New designed, compact mirrors reduce weight
- Slim new seat cowl.

*The 1998 ZX-6R – better by detail, rather than a major redesign.*

## 1998 ZX-6R G1/H1 Specifications

| | |
|---|---|
| Engine | Four-stroke, in-line four-cylinder |
| Displacement | 599cc |
| Bore and stroke | 68.0 × 43.8mm |
| Cooling | Liquid |
| Ignition | Digital |
| Starting | Eletric |
| Transmission | Six-speed |
| Frame | Pressed aluminium, perimeter |
| Suspension, front | 46mm cartridge fork with 12-way rebound, 10-way compression damping and spring preload adjustibility |
| Suspension, rear | Bottom-link UNI-TRAK with gas-charged shock, 20-way rebound, 20-way compression damping and spring preload adjustability |
| Tyre, front | 120/60 ZR17 T/L |
| Tyre, rear | 170/60 ZR17 T/L |
| Brakes, front/rear | Dual disk/single disk |
| Colour | Ebony/Pearl Chateau Gray, Lime Green/Metallic Violet Royal, Ebony/Firecracker Red, Sunbeam Red (N. America only). |

*A ZX-6R F2 (1996 model) being put through its paces.*

141

the Honda's 90.4bhp at 11,700rpm). Picking a winner – ZX-6R or CBR? If you're touring, there's nothing in it, although the Ninja's greater torque is important. Ride hard, and the differences depend more on where you're riding. On a track the Kawasaki demands more from the rider but rewards with quicker lap times. But on real roads the Honda comes out top . . . by a tiny margin.

And so we come to the final segment of the ZX Ninja trilogy, the new-for-1996 7R. And of the three, this had the most difficult mission. For a start it had to take over from the much-loved ZXR750, and at the same time offer a serious challenge in the world of Superbike racing. And if all that wasn't enough, it had to pinch as many sales as possible off a revised and even better Honda Fireblade. However, thanks to extensive research and input from the factory's world Superbike racing programme, the Ninja ZX-7R is a significant improvement over the machine it replaced.

At its heart is the heavily revised engine, displacing a total of 748.3cc – 73 x 44.7mm (compared to the ZXR's 71 x 47.3mm); and shorter, straighter inlet paths which improve combustion efficiency.

The new cylinder received a closed top-deck cooling system with wet liner that added strength to the cylinder, whilst offering additional cooling of the combustion chamber, especially in the critical centre region.

The offside cam chain was retained for a rigid, shorter crankshaft. Whilst in search for a more efficient overall engine design, a new direct actuation valve train (shim and bucket) was adopted to allow space for a steeper, more downdraught angle (50 degrees) for the carburettors.

With the new cylinder head featuring shorter, straighter inlet paths with an equally spaced carburettor pitch, volumetric efficiency was also improved. In addition, the design allowed a new centre pulley position for the carburettor throttle cables that offered the additional benefit of a lighter more positive throttle action.

*The ZX-7R replaced the ZXR750. This is the 1997 P2 version.*

*The more highly tuned, more single-purpose ZX-7RR. N1 model shown.*

In addition to making the inlet paths shorter, the new engine also featured narrower inlet ports (36mm) to boost inlet velocity; combined with the new, larger volume, twin ram air intake system, this resulted in improved cylinder charging and hence better volumetric efficiency, superior engine response and more mid-range power.

Carburettor size of the R (coded P) street-bike is 38mm, while the RR (coded N) racer employs four 41mm Keihin flat-slide instruments featuring a smooth bore to maximum air flow. The RR's carburettors feature an accelerator pump and fuel enricher.

Lubrication improvements over the ZXR included a plunger-type oil relief valve and a 30mm – deeper – oil pan. In addition, Kawasaki engineers made a substantial effort to decrease mechanical loss and oil stirring loss. Larger oil return passages between numbers two and three cylinders return more oil to the sump, whilst new equalizing passages balance the cylinder head and crankcase pressure for less resistance for the moving oil. Consequently reliability under the most demanding racing condition has also been increased.

Improvements to the cylinder head and the new wider bore required a new, stronger crank with stronger main journal support ribs.

Improvements to the transmission followed those already described for the ZX-6R – and again resulted in smoother, more positive gear changes and a greater mechanical reliability.

A curved aluminium radiator reduced the frontal area, whilst a new thermostat now actuated at a low 60°C (140°F) to help reduce mechanical loss due to excessive engine heat.

The 4-2-1 exhaust system features a balancer pipe between numbers one and four headers for improved mid-range power, whilst the exhaust's main collector pipe has a full diameter, unobstructed path to the larger-volume silencer for maximum high-speed exhaust flow.

As a point of further interest, the ignition igniter is programmed to interrupt the ignition for all four cylinders at 12,800rpm to prevent over-revving the engine, whilst the Kawasaki clean air system (KCAS) routes fresh air to the down-side of the exhaust port for cleaner exhaust emissions.

*The ZX-7R provided Kawasaki with a machine which could challenge for both showroom sales and racetrack success.*

Obviously with all the improvements to the engine, fresh attention also became necessary to other areas of the bike, so extensive computer-aided design (CAD) technology was undertaken to achieve an extra-rigid frame. The all-aluminium perimeter frame features 5mm larger frame rails, using the engine as a stressed member mounted in a diamond configuration. Rake and trail on the ZX-7R remain unchanged over the ZXR at 25 degrees and 99mm respectively. On the ZX-7RR, the rake and trail are adjustable.

Matching the improvements to the torsional rigidity of the chassis are upgraded suspension components. The all-new, completely adjustable, upside-down cartridge forks feature 43mm inner tubes with thinner, 2mm-thick walls. The ZX-7R (P) streetbike front forks feature adjustable spring preload, plus twelve-way rebound damping and eight-way compression-damping adjustability. The race-orientated ZX-7RR (N) fork sports thirteen-way rebound damping and twenty-eight-way compression damping, plus threaded spring preload adjustment.

Both versions feature a nitrogen gas-charged rear shock with 'piggy-back' reservoir, with spring preload adjusted by means of a threaded collar atop the shock. The P's shock has four-way rebound and twenty-way compression-damping adjustability, while that of the N comes with eighteen-way rebound and twenty-way compression-damping adjustability.

Rear ride height adjustment is via a threaded collar for the top shock mount; rear wheel travel is 130mm (5in).

Although the semi-floating 320mm front brake discs remain unchanged, a major improvement has come with the adaption of six-piston brake calipers. The solid rear disc measures 230mm (9in) in diameter, and is 6mm thick to reduce unsprung weight.

Adding to the race replica image are hollow, three-spoke, cast-aluminium wheels, the new 6in rear rim being able to take the very latest racing tyres. The front size remains unchanged at 3–5in.

New, low-profile ZR-17 tyres (front 120/70, rear 190/50) not only give extreme lean angles, but also help to reduce unsprung weight and increase tread life. The rear 190 is the widest motorcycle tyre currently available.

Compared to the ZX-6 and 9s, the 7 is instantly recognizable by its new fairing which features two separate headlamp apertures. The fairing also sports two massive intake scoops for the uprated, twin ram air system. To ease maintenance, the wiring harness is divided into front (cowling) and rear (frame) sections.

The ZX-7RR also comes with a close ratio gearbox, special clutch plates that have a paper-based material to absorb power and heat without deformation, an aluminium steering shaft, an adjustable swinging arm pivot, and of course a solo seat and no pillion footrests. Without the need to carry a passenger, the RR's aluminium rear subframe was designed to be lighter than the similar section device on the street-going ZX-7R.

In their May 1997 issue *Ride* magazine

compared the ZX-7R with the latest Suzuki GSX-R750W, and even though the Kwacker was 25kg (55lb) heavier than the Suzy, it was marginally faster at 167mph (269km/h) (the GSX-R achieved 163mph (262km/h). This was *Ride*'s verdict:

Ride a GSX-R750 in the sunshine on smooth, empty roads and you'll want one. My heart says buy one, but after two breakdowns my head says get the ZX-7R instead because it's just as good but in a different way. Not quite as raw and exciting, but not as scary or flimsy-feeling either. The Kawasaki is faster, better built, handles just as well on the road and looks the business too.

In 1998 the ZX-7R is unchanged, except colours and graphics.

*Having already created liquid-cooled fours for the 600, 750 and 900 classes, it was perhaps obvious that Kawasaki would expand its range to include the one-litre Superbike, and so for the 1986 model year the new GPZ1000RX took over from the air-cooled GPz1100.*

*The RX's 997cc (74 x 58mm) engine followed similar lines to the 900R.*

145

# KAWASAKI'S FIRST LIQUID-COOLED 1-LITRE – THE GPZ1000RX

Having already created liquid-cooled fours for the 600, 750 and 900cc classes, it was a virtual certainty that they would expand this formula to the prestigious 1-litre Superbike category, too. And so it came as no real surprise when just such a machine was announced in September 1985.

Reaching dealers early in 1986, the new model – coded GPZ1000RX – took over from the air-cooled GPz1000. The engine followed similar lines to the 900R, but with the bore and stroke increased from 72.5 x 55mm to 74 x 58mm, giving a displacement of 997cc. The 1000RX used flat-top aluminium pistons which, compared to the pentroof type, boosted combustion efficiency in this engine by an extra 1.3bhp. The compression ratio was 10.2:1.

The upper compression rings were a new type, with barrel faces and an inner bevel. Unlike conventional rings, the bevelled rings were designed to prevent 'flutter' at high piston speeds. Instead, each ring twisted slightly and wedged tightly between the top and bottom of its groove for significantly better sealing and increased durability.

Due to the increased stroke, piston speed at the 10,500rpm redline changed from 19.25 to 20.3m/s. Kawasaki engineers also carried out the following modifications over the 900R motor to ensure a high level of durability:

- Connecting rods were thicker and manufactured from stronger steel.
- Gudgeon pins were of a new type that offered increased strength with minimal weight.
- Big-end bolt diameter increased from 8 to 9mm. The valve timing was also changed (exhaust timing was unaltered).

- There were also new valves to increase airflow and reduce weight. For increased reliability, the head gasket was upgraded to stainless steel.
- The biggest news was an exclusive Kawasaki induction system that took advantage of the relatively cool, high-pressure airflow above the front of the engine. This sealed system featured two parallel ducts that extended forwards from the airbox to points just above and behind the radiator. Air entering the ducts was unheated by the radiator/engine, and was at relatively high pressure due to airflow off the fairing; thus it was denser than air in conventional systems. The insulated ducts directed the cool air over the cylinder head and into a larger, newly designed 7l (1fi gals) airbox for a significant power increase.

As on the air-cooled GPz750 and GPz1100, inlet ports were individually polished by senior Kawasaki technicians to further boost breathing efficiency. The company was the only Japanese manufacturer that applied such hand-craftmanship to production streetbikes at that time.

Another Kawasaki exclusive were the Keihan CVK 36mm instruments with semi-flat slides. These were larger than rival four-cylinder models, and the compact, aluminium-body carbs featured the same breathing efficiency at full throttle as conventional 38mm units, but delivered quicker response at smaller throttle openings (well, this was the theory – see later text). The carb downdraught angle was increased from 10 to 15 degrees, ensuring a straighter shot into the cylinders.

As for the exhaust system, the headers were now manufactured from corrosion-free stainless steel. Pipe diameter was up from 35 to 38.1mm compared to the 900R, but since stainless steel allowed single- rather than double-walled header construction, the complete 1000RX system weighed 2kg (4.4lb) less. The remainder of the exhaust however, including the collector box and silencers, was of mild steel construction, albeit with a dull chrome finish.

A variety of modifications to the liquid-cooling system increased maximum cooling capacity 25.5 per cent over the 900R to 19,700 Kcal/hr. The taller, narrower radiator measured 300 x 285 x 32mm (11.8 x 11.2 x 1.25in) and held 15.3 per cent more coolant. The diameter of the thermostat-controlled fan was up 38mm (1.5in) to 210mm (8.3in).

The cooling capacity of the new five-tier oil cooler was up 13.6 per cent to 2,500 Kcal/hr. The cooler measured 175 x 81 x 32mm (6.9 x 3.2 x 1.25in) and held 9.1 per cent more oil.

For improved starting, a stronger 7 per cent starter motor spun a higher-ratio idler gear.

The one-piece crankshaft turned in five plain bearings, with inserts made of the same alloy used in other liquid-cooled GPZ models. And in other areas, the 1000RX shared the technology with its older brother the 900R.

It was deemed necessary to uprate the clutch with the following modifications:

- The clutch basket (with 900R clutch gear) and hub (with cam damper) were adopted from the air-cooled 1985 GPz1100;
- the number of driving plates was increased from eight to nine;
- the driven plates were increased from seven to eight (and the thickness up from 1.6 to 2.3mm);
- the number of plate teeth were increased;
- the springs were increased from five to six;
- and finally, a longer input shaft accommodated the new clutch.

Inside the gearbox, all the teeth for third to sixth gears were now specially ground to increase efficiency and durability, and to reduce noise; while the dogs for third and fourth gears (in addition to fifth and sixth) were now undercut in an effort to provide more positive shifting.

Whilst internal ratios remained the same, the final drive ratio changed from 2.882 (49/17) on the 900R to 2.666 (40/15) on the

*The 1000RX was certainly an impressively engineered bike. Although its 163mph (262km/h) maximum speed allowed owners to boast in their 'local', on the road it was actually slower in A-to-B situations than the less powerful and lighter 900R.*

1000RX. Otherwise, as with the engine, the 1000RX's transmission shared components with the 900R.

In the chassis department, the new 1-litre Superbike used a new perimeter frame with a configuration somewhat similar to the 600R. Comprising a combination of high-tensile steel, mild steel and aluminium, this frame weighed only 20kg (44lb).

There were three separate frame components: a main section of box-section high-tensile and mild steels; a downtube section of box-section high-tensile steel; and a rear section of box-section aluminium. For increased rigidity, the downtubes were joined by a welded cross-brace into a single section, which was joined to the main section by eight bolts.

There were six engine mounts: two rubberized mounts at the downtubes, and four rigid mounts near the swinging arm pivot. In combination with the engine balancer system, this ensured exceptional smoothness for such a large, powerful (125bhp) machine.

The new bodywork had a similar appearance to the 600R, but although wider, had a lower drag coefficient. Next to increased power, this fairing was a major factor in the 10mph (16km/h) increase in maximum speed over the 900R. It is interesting to note that the full fairing reduced drag by 12 per cent compared to an unfaired bike, but the one on the 1000RX weighed only 3.64kg (8lb), making a total weight of bodywork of 9.15kg (20lb).

On the 1000RX there was an uprated Uni-Trak rear suspension. With a linkage that compressed the shock from both ends, this system provided increased wheel travel with reduced shock stroke, providing better distribution and allowing more freedom in selecting progressive suspension curves. There was also superior protection for the alloy linkage, which was equipped with low-friction needle bearings. The improved Uni-Trak also featured air-assisted and adjustable rebound damping.

Shock stroke was 62.5mm (down 2.5 from

*Famous for the endurance racing exploits of the 1970s, the French Godier & Genoud tuning house offered its own version of the RX: the ZRX1000. This was virtually an endurance racer on the road.*

900R), whilst rear wheel travel was 130mm (5in) – up 15 from 900R. The 1000RX also had the strongest swinging arm ever put on a production Kawasaki up to that time, its extruded box-section aluminium assembly measuring 27.5 x 60mm (1.08 x 0.39in).

The front fork with automatic variable damping system (AVDS) was based on that already in use in both the 900R and 600R, but with 40mm (1.5in) stanchions and different spring rates, compression damping and other more minor details.

The braking system, too, took much from the 900R, with the dual front discs being the same size as the smaller model (280mm diameter, 5mm thick). But the rear disc diameter was actually *smaller* – down 10mm to 260mm, although the thickness remained the same at 7mm. The single piston calipers utilized the same type of high-performance brake liners and improved sintered metal pads introduced on the 600R.

Valving in the adjustable anti-dive system had been modified for quicker response.

The 16in cast-aluminium wheels on the 1000RX were similar to those introduced on the 600R. The V-rated Bridgestone Excedra tyres were new, but based on those already in service on the 600R: whilst the 120/80 V16 front tyre was the same size as the 900R's, the large 150/80 V16 was a full 15.1 per cent wider for improved traction.

The 60/55-watt halogen headlamp and dual horns were taken from the 600R. Charged by a 350-watt alternator, the battery was rated at 12v 15amp/10hr.

With a fuel capacity of 21 litres (4⅝ gal), the 1000RX was well able to perform a sports/touring role, helped also by features such as a comfortable dual seat, retractable luggage cord hooks, a pair of helmet locks, and a newly devised passenger grab handle which could be retracted for solo riding.

Instrumentation was taken care of by an extra-large electric tacho and a smaller mechanical speedo. These were flanked by a fuel gauge and water temperature gauge, while all warning lights (turn signals, oil pressure, side stand etc) were lined up at the base of the instrument console.

Weighing in at 238kg (525lb) (dry) the 1000RX could hardly be described as anything other than heavyweight.

Maximum power of 124bhp was produced at 9,500rpm, with the standing 400m (¼ mile) being despatched in 10.6 seconds; maximum speed was 163mph (262km/h). All class-leading stuff for its time, but out on the road, and even more so on the track, the newcomer found itself unable to match the slower and lighter 900R from A to B. In other words, the 1000RX was difficult and demanding to ride in anything other than a straight line.

However, it does play a vital and important part of the Kawasaki liquid-cooled four-cylinder story, siring as it did both the ZX10 and the superb ZZ-R1100.

## ZX-10: MORE MUSCLE, LESS WEIGHT

The GPZ1000RX was replaced at the end of 1987 by the ZX-10. With more power, increased torque, higher speed (169mph/272km/h) and lighter weight, the ZX-10 took over the laurels as the 'world's fastest production roadster'. The 1000RX engine was carefully improved, rather than given a complete redesign. Engine component weight was cut wherever possible, amounting to an overall reduction of 4kg(8.8lb). The cylinder head was completely new: it featured an individual rocker valve train (based on that introduced on the GPX750) which reduced reciprocating mass (by 68 per cent) for increased redline and added reliability. The head also featured straighter, semi-downdraught inlet ports, which were again

*The 1000RX was replaced for the 1988 model year by the ZX-10. With 136bhp, increased torque and higher maximum speed (electronically tested at a shade under 170mph (274km/h), the ZX-10 took over the mantle as the 'world's fastest production roadster' from the 1000RX.*

hand-finished for maximum induction efficiency. A larger 8-litre (1flgal) airbox, semi-downdraught carbs (still 36mm), and an improved version of Kawasaki's much-trumpeted high-velocity induction system complemented the polished ports. More compact combustion chambers and a higher 11:1 compression ratio helped to maximize combustion efficiency, while lighter pistons and a lightened crankshaft/balancer allowed a 500rpm redline increase (to 10,000rpm) as well as improved reliability. Spark plug diameter was reduced from 12 to 10mm, whilst the upper piston ring thickness had been cut from 1mm to 0.8mm.

New steel connecting rods were some 15 per cent lighter, but the small-end diameter (18mm) and the lightweight, hollow, tapered gudgeon pins remained unchanged. The big-end diameter (35mm) was also unchanged, but oil clearance had been tightened 10 microns for increased film pressure and consistency, which ensured that bearing load at redline remained unchanged. Lighter, 8mm chrome-molybdenum bolts replaced the 1000RX's heavier 9mm components.

Due to the useful reduction in recipro-cating weight, piston speed at redline could be increased from 20.3m/s at 10,500rpm to 21.3m/s at 11,000rpm with no reliability loss.

Both inlet and exhaust valves (and ports) had been increased in size. The inlet valve head diameter was up 1mm to 30mm whilst exhaust valve diameter was increased by 1.3mm to 26mm. With a reduction in stem diameter by 0.5mm to 5mm, valve weight was virtually unchanged. Each stem was specially treated to increase durability.

The improvement in breathing efficiency was clearly evidenced by the fact that duration in the valve timing had been *decreased* despite the increased redline figure.

In what could be viewed as a retrograde step, the exhaust header pipes were now manufactured from single-wall mild steel, chrome-plated to help corrosion problems. Pipe diameter remained unchanged at 38.1mm.

The ZX-10's two cooling systems (water-based and oil) were improved versions of the 1000RX. The cooling capacity of the water-based system remained the same, but the new cylinder head featured larger passages directly over the combustion chambers which improved heat transfer in the important area.

Whilst oil is a far less efficient coolant than a water-based solution, it can cool otherwise inaccessible points. As in the 1000RX, the lubricant flowed through a dual-stage system. In the internal oil loop, oil was drawn through the primary filter to the pump, then passed through the filter element to the crank, gearbox, head etc. In the external loop, oil was passed from the pump to the cooler, then back to the sump.

The cooling capacity of the oil cooler remained unchanged, but larger rotors in the internal circuit pump (up 2mm to 14mm) increased output volume, which ensured increased oil pressure as compared to the 1000RX under hard-riding conditions. The rotors for the cooler circuit remained unchanged at 16mm.

A new sump pan increased total oil capacity by 0.25 litres (½ pint) to 4 litres (7 pints), which helped reduce oil temperature and thus increase pressure. Maximum oil pressure was $5kg/cm^2$. To minimize mechanical loss, the sump oil level was kept at a minimum whilst the engine was in operation, a special dam isolating the area around the balancer gear, primary gear and clutch.

Another improvement was the new digital system which provided a more precise advance curve. The single timing sensor was on the left (near) side end of the crankshaft. Other electrical improvements included an improved fuel pump and a new, lighter starter motor, and whilst peak output of the alternator had been slightly reduced by 10watts to 340, low rpm output had been significantly increased over that of the 1000RX.

Like the 1000RX, the ZX-10 drivetrain featured gear primary drive, hydraulically operated clutch and a six-speed gearbox. There was, however, a new clutch basket which was lighter and designed for quieter operation. Due to the reduced mass of moving engine components, the force exerted on the clutch during engine braking had been greatly reduced, therefore the cam damper fitted to the 1000RX was eliminated.

The nine driving plates were identical to the 1000RX's. To handle the increased power, the thickness of the six middle driven plates was up from 2.3 to 2.9mm, whilst the remaining two plates were up to 2.6mm.

Inside the gearbox, the teeth for second through to sixth gears were now specially ground to increase efficiency and durability and reduce noise (third through to sixth gears on the 1000RX). The dogs for third

*The ZX-10 was voted 'Machine of the Year' by readers of* Motor Cycle News, *1988.*

through sixth gears were still undercut for more positive shifts.

The ZX-10 had a 532 drive chain, in place of the 1000RX's 630 component.

In the area of chassis design, Kawasaki at last bowed to fashion and produced a new 'E-box' frame of extruded, dual-box-section aluminium. It was 4.5kg (9.9lb) lighter than the 1000RX's steel/aluminium item, and Kawasaki claimed that it also offered increased rigidity.

The new ZX-10 fairing not only had four major sections (instead of five on the 1000RX) but was 7 per cent more slippery than its predecessor. At 7.63kg (16.8lb), the complete fairing and bodywork weighed 0.72kg (1.6lb) less than the 1000RX's.

There was improved suspension, including 41mm (1mm up on 1000RX) forks, while stanchion wall thickness was down 0.5mm to 3mm. At the rear the Uni-Trak system remained largely unchanged, although grease nipples on the linkage eased maintenance.

The ZX-10 offered the first dual front-floating discs (300mm in diameter, therefore up 20mm) mounted on any Kawasaki street-bike. The rear (solid) disc was 250mm (down 10mm) and 6mm thick (down 1mm). The calipers were also different, with Kawasaki's balanced actuation calipers (BAC) introduced on the GPX750, with different-size pistons to

*In the area of chassis design, Kawasaki at last bowed to fashion and produced a new 'E-box' frame of extruded, dual-box-section aluminium.*

balance pressure and thus, it was claimed, to provide stronger stopping power, improved feel and better wear – or so Kawasaki claimed. Certainly they were an improvement over the 1000RX's twin piston affairs.

The combination of new 17 and 18in cast-aluminium wheels featuring large hollow hubs to maximize rigidity while minimizing unsprung weight, and new Dunlop K455 V280 tubeless tyres (120/70 VR17 front and 160/60 VR18 rear) with lower profile, ensured that overall wheel/tyre diameter – and thus gyroscopic effect – was similar to the 1000RX.

Attention to detail had also not been overlooked. There was a larger 22-litre ($4^7/8$ gal) fuel tank, whilst the one-piece dual seat was longer, wider and lower (the seat height was 790mm/31in against 805mm/32in on the 1000RX, making life easier for both rider and passenger alike. There were also new four-way clutch and brake lever adjusters, push-to-cancel turn indicators and improved instrument faces to ensure easier readability.

In combination with the lighter engine, the new chassis helped to reduce the overall dry weight to 222kg (489lb) – a full 16kg (35lb) lighter than the machine it replaced.

Not only did a ZX-10 win the Manx Grand Prix in 1988 (with Paul Hunt), it was also the UK's top selling over-750cc machine that year, with 1,060 units; next best was Honda's CBR1000 with 913 sold. But whilst undoubtedly fast, the ZX-10 was not an out-and-out sportsbike in the same way as the Yamaha FZR1000 or the Suzuki GSX-R1100. Instead it offered an almost unbeatable combination of usable power and two-up touring ability. The only flies in the ointment were an extremely annoying mid-range flat spot and somewhat over-heavy steering. Otherwise it was without doubt Kawasaki's best big bike yet and would remain so until the advent of its replacement, the much-lauded ZZ-R1100 which appeared as the 1990s replaced the 1980s.

## Modern GPZ1100 – Wolf in Sheep's Clothing

After the ZX-10 came the ZZ-R1100 (see Chapter 12). But there is another 1100, the GPZ. This is not based on the old air-cooled model of the same designation, but instead an all-new sports/tourer featuring a detuned ZZ-R motor.

Introduced in 1995, the 'new' GPZ1100 has hardly been a sales success. This is largely due to its uninspiring looks – like some 'gigantic GPZ500' as *Ride* said in their October 1995 issue. But behind the bland exterior it is an irritatingly well sorted all-rounder. Fast riding, town trickling, long-distance journeys, two-up touring – it does the lot, simply superbly. *Ride* again:

> It's so easy to walk up to the GPZ every morning, wipe the dew off the seat and go. That bare plastic console is festooned with real-world comforts – clock, fuel gauge, controllable choke, clear mirrors. You get room for a lock and one-piece oversuit under the seat, enough grunt between 4 and 6000 to waft past cars in high gears, and space for a tall pillion. Most deceptive of all, the Kawasaki goes nearly as fast on a twisty road as the Suzuki (RF900R) with half the effort, and leaves the Yamaha (FJ1200) behind.

*New for 1995, the GPZ1100. This owed nothing to the earlier air-cooled model of the same designation – instead it was a modern sports-tourer. The engine was based on the ZZ-R1100, but tuned for still more mid-range power. It was available with or without ABS.*

The ZZ-R-derived engine is quite heavily detuned. To provide additional torque in the 4–6,000rpm area it runs softer cams, breathes through smaller 36mm carbs and out through a different exhaust. Nothing awesome here. Against the ram-air ZZ-R's near 180mph (290km/h), the GPZ does a more comfortable 156mph (250km/h). But who really cares, as both will cruise comfortably at 130mph (210km/h), which must be enough for everyone except a GP road racer! And what the GPZ lacks in top end is more than compensated for by its ability to accelerate from rest.

Even though it has an old-fashioned steel frame, handling is surefooted and safe. And combined with 17in modern, low profile tyres and wide rims it can match many sports bikes.

The brakes are equally effective, although a £1,300 price premium for ABS (albeit with a pair of panniers thrown in) is not worth paying for. Only poor fuel consumption (averaging 38mpg (7.4l/100km) in *Ride*'s test) and those lack-lustre looks work against what is otherwise one of the most underrated bikes of the 1990s.

153

# 12   ZZ-R1100

Honda can boast of their Fireblade, Ducati of their 916, but for Kawasaki and its myriad fans around the world the bike which really stands at the head of 1990s Superbiking is the awesome ZZ-R1100. When the machine was first announced towards the end of 1989 it created a major stir throughout the industry, because here was a bike which set new standards, not just for the sports/touring class that it was so clearly aimed at, but it was also the fastest production roadster ever. It would have been an easy task for Kawasaki to have created a new flagship by simply taking the top selling ZX-10, boring it out a bit, adding a couple of styling changes and selling it at a higher price, but luckily this didn't happen.

The ZZ-R1100 (ZX-11 in the States) had an engine which featured several major changes to boost torque and strength. The chassis was new; so too were the bodywork, wheels, suspension, tyres and brakes. It also rectified the problems of mid-range flat spots and over-heavy steering which had affected its predecessor, the ZX-10. Kawasaki's design team created the ZZ-R very much as a sports-tourer, but with class-leading performance combined with the ability to corner with the best of them. In a 1990 *What Bike?* issue, tester John Nutting began by saying:

*The original ZZ-R1100C1 of 1990. At the time of its introduction it was the fastest series production streetbike which a major manufacturer had yet put on the market.*

Life is always full of surprises. And just when you thought that big, powerful motorcycles had to be awkward and unmanageable, along comes the ZZ-R1100. At a stroke, here's a motorcycle that rewrites the book on both performance and handling!

Although on paper the engine might have appeared to have been simply an overbored ZX-10, in reality there were a great many changes, primarily aimed at increasing volumetric efficiency. For a start, Formula 1 race-car type technology was introduced in the form of a new, forced induction system: this drew incoming air from an inlet port at the front of the fairing located below the headlamp, and this was fed via a sealed duct straight to the airbox. The fact that it was sealed (unlike any other production motorcycle model at the time) meant that there was no chance for the induction air to be heated by the radiator or engine. The air duct had also been so shaped that any rainwater would lie at the bottom and not be drawn into the carburettors. These latter components were 40mm (up from 36mm on the ZX-10) Keihin CVKD semi-flat-slide instruments,

fed by an electric fuel pump, with a duct from the forked induction system to compensate for increased airbox pressure.

The engine's bore size had been increased from 74 to 76mm compared to the ZX-10, giving a capacity increase of 55cc (a total displacement of 1,052cc). The whole block was tilted forwards 17 degrees (2 degrees more than the ZX-10) to allow as large a fuel tank capacity as possible as well.

The individual rocker arm valve train pioneered on the ZX-10 was retained, though exhaust diameter was up 1.5mm to 31.5mm, and the inlet by 1mm to 26mm. Both the inlet and exhaust ports were enlarged in line with the bigger valves, and as with the ZX-10 they were hand-finished to gain breathing efficiency. The valve timing had been changed to provide slightly longer duration.

The ZX-10's flat-topped pistons had been replaced by concave crown types, which despite the larger diameter actually weighed 12g (0.4oz) less, at 180g (6.4oz) each; this was achieved by reducing skirt height. Changing the con-rod material from carbon steel to chromium molybdenum steel with heat treatment allowed the rotating mass to be reduced without sacrificing strength.

*A ZZ-R1100D1 naked, showing the massive alloy beam chassis, giant sealed airbox, liquid-cooled engine and comprehensive exhaust.*

All these changes meant increased power – a mind-blowing 147bhp in unrestricted form (UK version 125bhp, Germany 100bhp, at launch). Just to put things into perspective, that was just 5bhp short of the 2.9 litre 4 x 4 Ford Sierra, 15 *more* than a 2-litre Vauxhall Cavalier SRi, and 24 more than the motorcycling fraternity's best car friend, the big Volvo. To handle all this extra 'go' of the unrestricted versions, the crankpin diameter was increased by 1mm to 36mm; also the addition of a torque limiter between the starter motor and crankshaft allowed for greater generator chain liability.

In the area of cooling/lubrication there was not only an increase in cooling capacity, but a curved radiator to replace the ZX-10's flat type, whilst improved lubrication was achieved by additional wet liner passages under the combustion chamber to improve heat dissipation in this vital area. The improved cooling helped to prevent pre-ignition, and the opportunity was taken to advance the timing of the digital ignition unit to keep the top-end torque curve fat.

Another important change was to the exhaust, where there was now a 4 into 1 into 2 type, a modification to improve the mid-range and top-end torque. By joining exhaust pipes one and four and two to three, plus carefully tuning pipe length to a special baffle, maximum advantage was taken of exhaust pulsation and scavenging effect. The result was reduced noise *and* increased torque throughout the whole rpm band.

Larger diameter clutch plates with radial grooving for the driven plates provided increased heat capacity and a great resistance to fade. A change of friction material meant smoother power delivery and longer service life. An added bonus was a lighter action.

The internal gear ratios remained unchanged from the ZX-10, but the primary reduction ratio had been lowered by 5 per cent. In the interests of additional strength, the material of the second, third and fourth input gears, plus second and third output gears, had been upgraded from chromium to nickel chromium molybdenum steel, whilst additional lubrication had been provided for the shift forks.

Although visually similar to the ZX-10s, the frame nonetheless featured a number of important changes, not the least being that the wall thickness of the double box-section all-aluminium perimeter frame had been increased by 0.8mm, and the swinging arm pivot had been redesigned to give a smooth external face. The extra wall thickness, plus a new (aluminium) swinging arm with dual box-section construction, increased chassis rigidity, especially torsional.

Dimensional changes were restricted to the caster angle being reduced half a degree to 26 degrees, with the trail being upped 2mm to 103mm. The wheelbase was shorter by 10mm at 1,480mm (58.2in).

The whole frame was coated with a specially formulated finish to give not only a longer-lasting gloss, but superior protection from corrosion.

At the front end the forks were all new, with the stanchion diameter up to 43mm (the wall thickness was reduced to 2.5mm to avoid increasing the weight) to provide extra stiffness. At the rear a new, aluminium-bodied, remote reservoir, nitrogen-charged shock absorber was used for the by now familiar Uni-Trak rear suspension to provide improved fade resistance.

Braking had similarly been improved. Up front, a pair of 310mm (272mm on the ZX-10) semi-floating discs were each gripped by a four-piston caliper, while at the rear there was a dual-piston caliper for the single 250mm disc, with a frame-mounted torque arm. *What Bike?* tester John Nutting was obviously impressed with the highly improved ZZ-R1100 stopping power:

## Double Ton-plus Record

In March 1966, Mike Grainger, a Plymouth-based Kawasaki dealer, set a new official European bike speed record when he averaged 209.05mph (336.36km/h) over the flying quarter mile (400m) on his turbocharged ZZ-R1100, at Elvington, north Yorkshire. The ex-RAF airfield was hired specially for the occasion. His first run was into a strong headwind which kept the speed to just 205.47mph (330.60km/h), then later he made another run in the opposite direction to record a speed of 212.76mph (342.33km/h) – the average of 209.05mph (336.36km) beat the old record by nearly 9mph (14.5km/h); this had been set on a purpose-built, fully streamlined machine powered by a Norton rotary engine.

By contrast, Mike Grainger's machine was fully road-legal – in fact it looked just like any other ZZ-R1100, apart from its bright yellow, blue and white livery. What was less obvious was that it had been kitted out with an American-made 'Mr Turbo' turbocharger and fuel injection system, which more than doubled the power output. To cope with this vast increase in power there was a 40mm longer swinging arm, plus a ZX-10 rear wheel. The purpose of this latter component was that at 18in instead of the ZZR's 17in rim size, the gearing was raised to compensate for the extra speed. With only a 0.6 mile (1km) run-in, the machine was still accelerating as it passed through the ACU-operated timing lights . . . indicating that an even higher speed was possible.

*In March 1996 Mike Grainger, a Plymouth Kawasaki dealer, set a new European motorcycle speed record of 209.05mph (336.36km) on his road-legal, turbocharged ZZ-R1100.*

You can't get much better than that, and it all performs to perfection. Immensely powerful, the brakes can be controlled perfectly precisely, even while cranked over.

To keep this very considerable level of performance potential in check, the ZZ-R1100 placed a wide footprint on the tarmac, the V-rated radial tyres measuring no less than 120/70–17 front, 170/60–17 rear. The wheels they graced were of a three spoke design, with hollow hubs for lower unsprung weight.

The 1990 C1 version in unrestricted 147bhp guise gave a maximum speed of around 176mph (283km/h). And all this with a fuel economy some 30 per cent better than Yamaha's FJ1200! During 1990 the world's motorcycling press voted the ZZ-R1100 'International Bike of the Year', as did the readers of several journals around the world,

*April 1990. After serving as Kawasaki Motors UK managing director for four years, Shiuji Mihara (left) welcomes his successor, Yasuo Akisade. Under Mihara's leadership, the new ZZ-R1100 had been launched successfully into the important British market.*

including the top selling *Motor Cycle News*. One journalist seemed to echo all the others by saying:

> The five stars say it all. And even if the ZZ-R1100 could clock no more than 150mph [240km/h] the conclusion would be the same: it's the best of the heavyweights by far. Having stunning top speed just adds to the image. In these days of increased specialization, it comes as a surprise to find a machine which has both stunning performance and good road manners, which at once can shock its rider with both its speed and level of refinement. It may sound corny to say that I was sorry to give the bike back to Kawasaki, but I was, and I haven't experienced that feeling for a long time. By my reckoning the ZZ-R1100 is easily the bike of 1990?

Of course there was also the not insignificant fact that the ZZ-R1100 was the world's fastest production roadster . . . 176mph (283km/h) (in unrestricted guise). And except for an update for the 1993 season in the shape of the D1 model, the ZZ-R1100 has remained surprisingly unchanged, proving how near the mark it was first time.

The D1 changes included twin instead of single ram-air intake, refinement of the engine to capitalize on the advantages of the pressurized intake system, and increased overall breathing efficiency. There were larger diameter, larger volume silencers which permitted higher flow rates while meeting stringent exhaust noise regulations.

An all-new aluminium perimeter frame benefited from technology gleaned from the company's ZXR World Super Bike racing programme. There was also a new alloy cast section for the suspension link pick-up/swinging arm pivot which increased rigidity in that area.

New, larger 320mm front discs offered a greater swept area for improved braking performance, whilst at the rear a new, fatter 180/55–17 tyre gave even more grip.

*For 1993, Kawasaki introduced the updated D1 model. This featured twin ram-air induction, all-new chassis and a larger 24-litre (5¼ gal) fuel tank.*

*Other changes on the ZZ-1100D1 included larger 320mm front discs, flush-fitting inner fairing cowling, modified exhaust and a dry weight of 233kg (514lb) (against 228kg (503lb) of the C variant).*

Extensively tested in the factory's wind tunnel for an efficient profile with a low drag coefficient, the redesigned fairing offers the twin benefits of a more sporting image but with superior weather protection. This latter requirement was also assisted by a new, taller, wider windscreen which directed more wind blast around the rider whilst the wider frontal area of the fairing body afforded greater protection for the rider's hands. Other details saw a new tail section with integrated rear turn signals, a new type of fuel gauge, and other more minor changes.

Since 1993 the ZZ-R1100 has remained unchanged, although from November 1996 onwards UK models have been brought in with power upped from 125 to 147bhp. The 1997 model is coded D5. Also in late 1996 the new Honda Super Blackbird appeared on the scene ready to snatch the ZZ-R1100 'faster' crown. The designer's brief was to produce a 187.5mph (300km/h) bike, but early tests seem to question if this has in fact been achieved.

So although there is some uncertainty as to whether in fact Honda or Kawasaki has the crown, the fact remains that the ZZ-R is still right up there, even after more than seven years – and that is quite some record in itself in the modern world.

# 13 Endurance Racing

Endurance racing is able to trace its origins right back to the very beginnings of motorcycling. Well before the end of the nineteenth century, several French-based individuals had created organizations to explore the use of the yet untried Otto-cycle engine, and this created a fledgling motorcycle industry. These early pioneers included men such as the Count de Dion and his mechanic Georges Bouton, Maurice Fournier, Ernest Michaux and Félix Theodore Millet. In addition, the Russian-born brothers Eugène and Michel Werner had settled in France and become Frenchmen through adoption. All these men had a hand in placing France at the very forefront of motorcycle development as the twentieth century began.

The first recorded endurance race was the Paris–Dieppe event of 1897. Early feats of endurance were usually staged over public roads, and as time went by these point-to-point races became longer. And so it went on, and as the first decade of the new century unfolded, these events soon spread out from French borders. For example, the Paris–Prague of 1907 was a truly breathtaking feat, spanning as it did the entire expanse of continental Europe. Soon there were similar long-distance events in both America and Australia. The sheer sizes of both these countries lent themselves to epic record-breaking runs, ones of particular note being the 1,685-mile (2,711km) Three Flags classic from Canada to Mexico, and the Denver to Chicago, the latter over some 1,250 miles (2,011km) of largely dirt roads. There was also the epic coast-to-coast journey.

## THE BOL D'OR

What was to become the most famous long-distance race of all was launched in France during 1922. With a total of twenty-eight entries in its first year, the Bol d'Or was to grow into one of France's premier sporting occasions. This first Bol was held at Vaujours, and the winner was Zind, riding a 500 Motosacoche – and endurance racing as we know it today can trace its origins back to this inaugural race. Earlier events were for more specialized racing machinery, or simply a form of long-distance trial, rather than a road race. In addition, most events prior to the outbreak of the Great War in 1914 were staged over dirt, rather than tarmac roads.

The development of endurance racers has always tended to go hand-in-hand with street-going machines and the general basics of motorcycling. Over the years roadsters have ultimately benefited from endurance racing, as new developments tend to take place on the track first before the next generation of products appears in the showrooms. And as roadsters improve, the endurance racers are provided with better performance, handling, braking and reliability to withstand the rigours of twenty-four hours of non-stop abuse. As well as prototypes eventually being put into production, details such as tyres, suspension, brakes, chains and even electrical components have all been improved over the years. Thus the endurance racing machine has actually been responsible for many advances in ordinary motorcycles: the fact is that, although the

pukka grand prix bikes grab the big headlines, it is the endurance racers which do much of the real testing which benefits the bike-buying public.

Although other countries have attempted to compete with the French, the Bol d'Or remains the premier endurance event of the year. Even so, many have provided excellent events over the years: for instance, Belgium has Spa, Holland – Zolder, Japan – Suzuka, Spain – Barcelona, Great Britain – Thruxton, and Sweden – Anderstorp. The very first Bol d'Or saw motorcycles racing non-stop for forty-eight (yes, *forty-eight!*) hours. This was then followed by a similar event for cycle-cars and sidecars, this extravaganza lasting from the 22–29 May 1922. This event was held a year before the first twenty-four-hour car race at Le Mans, so it may be said that *bikes* actually began the French passion for long-distance circuit racing.

After the initial event at Vaujours, St Germain was the Bol's home, from 1923 through to 1936 (except 1927, when it was staged at Fontainebleau). Then in 1937 it moved to the legendary Montlhéry course. During the inter-war period, besides the original Motosacoche success, victory was secured by nine other makes (including Sunbeam, FN, Velocette, Norton and Motobécane).

Postwar, and the Bol d'Or was reinstated at St Germain in 1947, where it was won by Gustave Lefèvre on a plunger-framed International Norton. Lefèvre went on to record another six victories, the last one in 1957, making him the most successful rider in Bol D'Or history.

As the 1960s dawned, a general depression hit the motorcycle business, and there were only thirty-one starters for the 1960 Bol D'Or, from which only ten teams were still in circulation at the end of twenty-four hours. This lack of entries unfortunately resulted in a depressingly meagre number of spectators, and the financial loss meant that there was no Bol d'Or race from 1960 to 1968.

*Kawasaki GP star Kork Ballington with the French Kawasaki Performance team bike during the Bol d'Or, 18 September 1979.*

## ENTER THE SUPERBIKE

What saved the event – and most probably endurance racing in general – was the advent of the modern Superbike in the shape of Honda's CB750 and Kawasaki's magnificent Z1. It was very much a case of oriental fours to the rescue. Although the event was reborn in 1969, it was not until 1973 and the arrival of a mass of official factory machinery that the famous French endurance race was truly reborn. That year also marked the debut in the Bol d'Or of Kawasaki's then-new 903cc Z1, ten of which were in the race programme, including factory machines entered via the French importers, SIDEMM. These latter bikes came complete with factory mechanics and 'Pops' Yoshimura Junior.

Lined up against the Z1s were a host of interesting bikes including the new Yamaha XS750 triple, the TZ350 two-stroke twins, a pair of Suzuki 750 Daytona triples, John Player Nortons, BMWs, Laverdas, Moto Guzzis and no less than fourteen Hondas, including the race-winning 969cc Jap-Auto entry. Although a BMW finished third, all

*A tank-off shot of a Performance team bike during 1977. Note the use of 'slick' racing tyres.*

*French police-entered Z1000 endurance racer competing in a Bol d'Or at the end of the 1970s as a private entry.*

the others on the leaderboard were Kawasakis. If this had been forgotten by the time the next Bol d'Or came around, everyone was to receive a reminder because 1974 was to be the year of Godier/Genoud and Big K. Replacing their Honda engines for a Z1 unit, this team used a Swiss Egli chassis. The G and G entry not only went on to complete a longer distance than anyone had covered before in Bold d'Or history, it also chalked up further victories in the Barcelona Twenty-Four-Hour, the 1,000km at Mettet in Belgium, and was runner-up in the Spa Twenty-Four-Hour race. All this success meant that they were crowned FIM Coupe d'Endurance champions – effectively meaning a world title for Kawasaki.

More success came in 1975 for Godier/Genoud and Kawasaki, with another win at the Bol d'Or, this time with the engine capacity upped to 1,100cc. The factory also played its part, providing the most comprehensive team back-up ever seen in endurance racing. This was to pay golden dividends, with the marque grabbing the top three places that year. Interestingly the winning Kawasaki of Godier and Genoud featured a brand-new chassis designed by

Pierre Douaque and Michel Lambert. Much effort was devoted to designing a package with endurance events very much in mind: as well as a low weight, minimum frontal area, sure-footed handling and 'brackwall' stopping power, the design took into account such vital considerations as ease of maintenance, sufficient ground clearance, rider comfort and general reliability of the machine.

As in the previous year, during 1975 the Godier and Genoud Kawasaki didn't just win at the Bol d'Or, but set new records and standards wherever the team appeared; thus Kawasaki dominated the endurance world for two whole years. Stung into action, other makers fought back, notably Honda and Ducati, and so Kawasaki found the going much more difficult in the latter half of the 1970s. Technology and a multi-million pound budget finally brought Honda the success it craved – but even this approach was to be challenged in the 1980s, as a new breed of endurance racer came onto the scene.

## PERFORMANCE KAWASAKI

Honda forged a link with fuel giants Elf, which resulted in much new innovation; but whilst the Honda-Elf project was in its infancy, rivals Kawasaki were making up for lost time. The FIM had introduced the World Endurance Championship in 1980 (which had been won by Honda). However, all this was set to change, with Kawasaki in association with Serge Rosset, boss of the French Performance company, dominating the series in 1981 and 1982.

The two vast Performance trucks soon became a focal point of the endurance paddock. Containing sufficient facilities to feed and sleep twenty-plus staff as well as a superbly equipped workshop, Rosset's team transporters were a visual sign of his total commitment to gaining success. With

*Jacques Cornu at the 1982 Bol d'Or. He was joint World Endurance champion that year with Jean Chemarin riding one of the Performance Kawasaki machines.*

*One of the two vast Performance team trucks which became such a focal point of the endurance racing scene during the early 1980s.*

additional sponsorship from KVAS oils and KOOL cigarettes, absolutely no effort (or expense!) was spared in building up what was, even by GP standards, one of the most professional and well structured teams ever seen anywhere in motorsport.

In contrast to the Honda-Elf avant-garde approach, Kawasaki-Performance bikes were almost conventional in their design and appearance. The Performance-designed chassis was constructed from chrome-moly tubing, bronze-welded, with a cast-alloy, substantially ribbed swinging arm for the Uni-Trak rising-rate rocker-arm ATZ single rear shock absorber.

At the front a pair of 40mm Kyaba forks, of similar construction to the type used by Kork Ballington's KR500 four-cylinder two-stroke GP machine, ran in tapered, roller-head bearings. A mechanical anti-dive system (again from the KR500), first seen on a BMW Superbike built in the USA in 1976 by Udo Geitl and Todd Schuster, worked by relaying the braking force from the twin 350mm front discs, via a system of pivots and rods, to the fork crowns. It was an effective, although slightly heavier way of achieving front anti-dive than the hydraulic valving systems used by the other Japanese manufacturers.

*One of the Performance machines. The design was built around the Z1000J road engine, since endurance racing rules called for machines using production-based engines up to 1,000cc. Power output was 135bhp.*

*Jean Chemarin, joint 1982 World Endurance Champion.*

Although 18in wheels front and rear were occasionally fitted, mostly a 16in (Campagnolo) and 18in (Dymag) were standardized. Dunlop tyres were used exclusively by the Rosset team, providing excellent grip and wear properties, both of which are vital in endurance events. Chain adjustment was taken care of by eccentric blocks in the rear of the swinging arm and integral with the axle.

With rules stating that engines must be based on the then existing TT Formula 1 – using production-based four-strokes up to 1,000cc, or 600cc two-strokes – with external engine cases unmodified in any way, the engine chosen was built around the Z1000J roadster unit. This air-cooled, across-the-frame four was specially tuned by Performance themselves. They fitted their own design of camshafts to the 69.4 x 66mm, two valves per cylinder motor, paying particular attention to gas-flowing and porting of the head. The ports were opened out and oversize valves fitted, with twin-plug ignition and 34mm smoothbore Mikuni carburettors.

*Chemarin/Cormu/Pellandini, Bol d'Or 1982. They finished second, covering 2,238 miles (3,600km) at an average speed of 93.42mph (150km/h).*

*Just some of the spare parts which the Performance team kept in their pit: during the twenty-four hours of non-stop action, almost anything might have been needed.*

*The Performance-designed, cast-alloy, massively ribbed swinging arm for the Uni-Trak rising rate rocker-arm rear suspension. This employed a single ATZ hydraulic unit.*

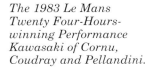

*The 1983 Le Mans Twenty Four-Hours-winning Performance Kawasaki of Cornu, Coudray and Pellandini.*

The crankshaft was welded up for extra stiffness, whilst the generator was relocated from its traditional home at the end of the crankshaft, to a new location atop the gearbox. Driven by a toothed rubber belt, it charged the battery which was positioned just in front of the rear wheel, beneath the rear shock. All this meant that the width of the engine was decreased, providing additional ground clearance, once again an endurance racing modification which would find its way through to a new generation of roadsters which Kawasaki was then in the process of designing.

Running on a compression ratio of 10.8:1, the Performance Kawasaki reliably put out 135bhp at 10,000rpm. This six-bearing crankshaft, using roller big ends and plain small ends, proved more than capable of lasting the full twenty-four hours and beyond without any sign of trouble.

There was a choice of three combinations for the second and third gears in the five-speed transmission, depending on the exact circuit and individual rider requirements.

For the rest of the 1980s Kawasaki went very much back to the development stage, with work taking place on the new liquid-cooled models. This largely left the endurance glory to their Japanese rivals. However, starting with the new GPX750, Kawasaki began to make a return later in the decade – and when the ZXR replaced the GPX, this effort moved into overdrive.

*One of the 1983 machines at the Silverstone world endurance round.*

*Kawasaki France GPX750 endurance racing squad, 1987.*

*The British Phase One ZXR750 team, one of the very few private teams to gain an endurance race victory counting towards the world title during the last decade.*

## THE 1990s SUCCESS STORY

Kawasaki France has continued its extremely active support of endurance racing on behalf of the Japanese parent company. This has seen considerable success, the highlights coming in 1992 and again in 1996, with the ultimate glory being victory in the world endurance championships. Rather conversely these titles have been carried off by British rather than French riders, in 1992, under the old rules which allowed *two* champions, Carl Fogarty and Terry Rymer, whilst in 1996 it was the Scot Brian Morrison. As we all know, Fogarty went on to add the WSB (World Super Bike) crown to his list of world titles (having also won the Formula 1 championship back in 1988).

As is recounted in Chapter 11 in the ZXR-750 story, both the endurance and WSB racing efforts were closely based around the ZXR-750 streetbike back in 1992, but by the time Morrison claimed his title the action had switched to the new ZX-7. There is no doubt that both racing series are

*Scotsman Brian Morrison, World Endurance Champion 1996, riding a factory ZX-7.*

of significant benefit to the ordinary road rider, in a way that grand prix racing can never be, and as such it is easy to justify Kawasaki withdrawal from the latter during the early 1980s. Because of this, Kawasaki's are likely to remain strong contenders in both the endurance and the WSB series, with a more focused approach than their Japanese rivals Honda, Suzuki and Yamaha, who also have to devote considerable time, effort and money to the grand prix arena.

*Morrison in action during the Le Mans Twenty-Four-Hour race, April 1996.*

# 14  WSB

Kawasaki quit Grand Prix road racing at the end of 1982. This was for several reasons, most notably the worldwide downturn in sales of standard production models during the early 1980s and the fact that the company was selling mainly four-strokes, whilst its GP racers were two-strokes.

During its last eight years of Grand Prix glory (1975–82), Kawasaki had developed several innovative features, including Uni-Trak rear suspension, air-adjustable front suspension and Electro Fusion cylinder bores. From then on the Team Green racing effort was centred on motocross and what was ultimately to emerge as World Super Bike (WSB) racing; with, of course, a continued participation in the more specialized world of endurance racing (outlined in Chapter 13).

The World Super Bike (WSB) series began in 1988, but in the United States the basic formula and Superbike name had been used during the preceding five years or so, bringing such names to prominence as Freddie Spencer, Eddie Lawson, Wayne Rainey and Kevin Schwantz – who all went on to become GP World Champions in the all-important blue riband 500cc category.

It was the Americans who really pushed the boat out to convince the FIM (the sport's international body) that Superbikes were vital to the future of racing. Early backers for the World Super Bike Championship concept were the legendary France family, owners of Daytona International Speedway, who provided the original series 'salesman', Californian Steve McLaughlin, with much of his initial help to say nothing of financial support.

It was agreed at the FIM's Paris Congress in October 1987 to run the first WSB championship during the 1988 season. The first-ever round of the new series was staged at Donington Park, England, in April 1988, where Ducati rider Marco Lucchinelli set the racing world on fire with a sensational victory aboard one of the booming Italian V-twins. Basically, the WSB rules allowed for 750cc fours and 1000cc twins, both with their own weight limits; later, a new rule was to be introduced which would allow 900cc three-cylinder machines.

Three main contestants emerged from that first year: Ducati with their water-cooled, fuel-injected, eight-valve V-twin; fellow Italians Bimota with the Yamaha OW01-engined YB4; and the V-four Honda RC30. At the year's end it was the combination of American Fred Merkel and the RC30 which came out on top against Italy's Davide Tardozzi on the Bimota. Lucchinelli took third, even though he didn't contest all the rounds.

Up until then the New Zealand-based Sports Marketing Company had largely funded the project, but with only days to go until the first race in the 1989 title chase (with the initial round again at Donington Park) they pulled the plug. The day was saved by the Japanese Moto Co., backed by the world's largest advertising agency, Dentsu. Then, a year later, European road race promoter Maurizio Flammini stepped in with a rival package which stole the WSB contract from under the noses of the Japanese. Subsequently a joint agreement was reached between the Italian and Japanese companies which saw the Flammini Group handling the day-to-day administration of the series and Dentsu the television production and distribution.

## EARLY DAYS

Kawasaki's first involvement in WSB came in 1989 with a very much toe-in-the-water approach. However, 1990 saw the company's presence rise through the Team Kawasaki Australia *équipe*, who came to Europe with their number one rider, Rob Phillis, who, in only three 1989 outings, had amassed enough points to secure joint tenth position in the championship table. For 1990 Phillis was partnered by New Zealander Aaron Slight (then beginning his career) and former Yamaha star Michael Dowson. However, although Phillis finished the season in fourth overall, it was American Doug Chandler, riding for the Team Muzzy squad, who really impressed,

winning both the USA and Japanese rounds.

For 1991 Kawasaki introduced the much improved ZXR750R(K). Rob Phillis responded with third overall, making him the highest non-Ducati rider. It is also worth mentioning that, in the AMA (American Motorcycle Association) Supersport national championship, Scott Russell was unbeaten with nine wins from nine races. In Britain John Reynolds finished third in both the Supercup and Superbike national championships. Whilst in Canada Steve Crevier won both the 750cc Production and Superbike national titles. Finally, Aaron Slight also took a double, in Australia, winning the Pan Pacific Superbike and Australian Superbike championships.

1992 began in fine style with Scott Russell winning the legendary Daytona 200 at record speed; this also being the first time that Kawasaki had won the event. Rob Phillis again finished third in the WSB series – again the first non-Ducati home. In Britain, John Reynolds had a stunning year, winning both the Supercup and Superbike championships.

*The 1993 WSB World Champion, Team Muzzy rider Scott Russell; ZXR 750.*

**1996 ZX-7RR Specifications**

| | |
|---|---|
| Engine | Four-stroke, DOHC in-line four-cylinder, 16 valves |
| Displacement | 748cc |
| Bore and stroke | 73.0 x 44.7mm |
| Cooling | Liquid |
| Carburettor | Keihin FVKD41 x 4* |
| Ignition | Digital |
| Transmission | Six-speed |
| Frame | Aluminium perimeter |
| Rake/trail | Adjustable 25 degrees/99mm |
| Suspension, front | Inverted 43mm cartridge fork with preloaded adjustment, 13-way adjustable rebound damping and 28-way compression damping adjustment |
| Suspension, rear | UNI-TRAK® with remote-reservoir shock threaded preload adjustment, 18-way rebound damping and 28-way compression damping adjustment |
| Wheel travel, front | 119.3mm (4.7in) |
| Wheel travel, rear | 129.5mm (5.1in) |
| Tyre, front | 120/70 ZR 17 tubeless radial |
| Tyre, rear | 190/50 ZR 17 tubeless radial |
| Brakes, front/rear | Dual disc/single disc |
| Seat height | 790mm (31.1in) |
| Dry weight | 200kg (441lb) |
| Fuel capacity | 21.8 litres (4.8 gal) |
| Wheelbase | 1420mm (55.9in) |

*Race kit options include FVKD 41 or FVKD 39 carburettors.

## KAWASAKI TRIUMPHANT

Then came Kawasaki's year, when Scott Russell became the first, and so far the only, Kawasaki rider to win the WSB title (otherwise it's been very much a Ducati and Honda benefit). His factory ZXR750 set a blistering pace that even the Ducati V-twins couldn't live with that year. To add to this WSB success Russell also – with Aaron Slight – won the prestigious Suzuka Eight-Hour race in Japan and was runner-up at Daytona.

The American then followed this up with victory in the 1994 Daytona 200 and after one of the most fiercely contested WSB series ever, against Ducati's new signing, Carl Fogarty, the Team Muzzy Kawasaki had to relinquish his treasured No. 1 plate, though

*When Scott Russell became WSB (World Superbike) champion in 1993 he rode for the American Muzzy-Kawasaki squad. The man behind Team Muzzy is the flamboyant Rob Muzzy.*

its fate was never certain until the very last round.

After the ZXR750 had turned in so many major championship wins worldwide since its conception five years earlier, the 1995 race season was one of mixed blessings. Though the season started well with Scott Russell again winning at Daytona, his departure to 500cc Grand Prix racing deprived Kawasaki of the chance of WSB success, though Jockhim Schmidt won the important German Pro Superbike series. The second Team Muzzy rider, the young Australian Anthony Gobert, showed the now ageing ZXR still had the ability to win races at World Championship level – indeed he demonstrated this in impressive style at the very last meeting of the 1995 series – but it was clear that Kawasaki would need a replacement machine, and sooner rather than later.

And that's just what happened with the ZX-7R being named as its replacement on both road and track for 1996. Rob Muzzy was again the man in charge, with his Muzzy team being Kawasaki's official representative in the World Super Bike series. For 1996 the

*One of Muzzy's more recent signings was the talented Australian youngster, Anthony Gobert, who produced some outstanding performances for the team in 1996.*

*Gobert, a truly gifted racing star combined skill with excitement like no one else on the circuit*

squad had two riders, Gobert and New Zealander Simon Crafar, both campaigning the all-new ZX-7RR. Crafar had been a consistent top ten finisher in the 1995 WSB series and had ended the season sixth in the points table. Crafar's consistency over Gobert's more flamboyant approach paid off, with the New Zealander finishing seventh in the 1996 championship, with Gobert back in ninth.

## NEW FACES FOR '97

The big news in 1997 was that Kawasaki's WSB team would now come under new management, in the shape of the German Harald Eckl, who was well known throughout the racing world with nearly twenty-two year's experience of the GP circuit as both a rider and team manager. In fact, only Simon Crafer remained from the

*Another Muzzy 1996 teamster was the vastly experienced New Zealander, Simon Crafar, seen here on one of the team's ZX-7Rs.*

*Terry Rymer and Ian MacPherson (shown) are the official Kawasaki entries in the 1997 British Superbike Championship series, riding Factory-kitted ZX-7RRs.*

previous year. Team Muzzy retreating back to the States and AMA Superbike racing, whilst Anthony Gobert switched to Grand Prix. Crafar was joined by a new rider: the exciting Japanese, Akira Yanagawa. With the latest ZX-7RR benefiting from further developments, a reorganized team line-up and new management, Kawasaki's aim is to recapture the series championship it last held in 1993. But realistically, much of the planning was for a serious bid in 1998, rather than 1997. By then the new squad should be a more settled force.

Whilst all this was going on Kawasaki's domestic All-Japan Superbike management and machine development had been combined to create a single team effort. The factory, with its development riders Akira Ryo and Sinya Takeishi, under the guidance of manager Takaski Yasai, not only gave Kawasaki a real chance of winning the 1997 Japanese championship, but carried out vital development work which would benefit the WSB effort in the future.

Perhaps Kawasaki's businesslike but friendly approach to its racing efforts is best illustrated by a letter sent to the company's distributors around the world. Dated 27

*For 1997 Muzzy went back to AMA (American Motorcycle Association) racing, whilst the factory entrusted its WSB effort to the German Harald Eckl. He retained Crafar and also signed the exciting Japanese newcomer, Akira Yanagawa.*

December 1996, it concludes: 'We hope to be reporting to you throughout the new year with lots of winning news. Thank you all for your successful efforts during 1996 and good luck with your racing programs in 1997. Happy holidays. Let the Good Times Roll!'

There's no doubt that Good Times and World Super Bike go together, and why not another Kawasaki world title soon, to add to the one it took back in 1993?

As if to confirm that a more serious challenge can be expected in 1998, Akira Yanagawa scored his first WSB victory at the Austrian round of the 1997 championship at the Österreichring in August 1997.

## 1997 ZX-7RR Race Kit

### Basic Kit for Engine Performance
New for 1997. Part No. 99996-1201 Cost: £5,424 (ex sales tax)

Includes: Camshafts, valves, valve springs, sprocket for adjustable valve timing, cam tensioner, pistons, piston rings, rod assembly, clutch housing (to reduce friction), clutch springs, input shaft, carburettor kit, oil pump, ignition components including CDI and ignitor, spark plugs, gaskets, shims and other small parts. 1997 Manual (English), part no. 99929-XXXX, is separate, costing £59.72.

### Other Race Kit Parts (cycle)

Include:Fuel tank complete (for kit Ram Air Case 24l)
      Mountings for fuel tank
      Ram air filter casing, upper and lower
      Smaller components for above
      Cowling ducts for ram air intake
      Muffler body (102db)
      Complete exhaust assembly (improved performance)
      Glass wool kit (meets 1997 regulations)
      Mounting kit for exhaust
      Chassis setting components
      Suspension
      Riding position adjustment
      Steering damper
      Marchesini wheels
      Brembo brakes
      Front mudguard
      Alternate sprockets 37 to 44T inclusive

There are also a vast range of transmission options, carburettor options, a more efficient cooling system (including upper and lower radiators and some magnesium parts to reduce weight), not to mention the new-for-1997 gear-driven camshaft system.

## What's New – 1997 & 1998 ZX-7RR Racing Kit Parts

### A. Basic Kit

#### Cylinder Head

- 1-8   92055-1509   O-ring: Decreasing of the number of O-rings for ASV-pipe, from 12 to 8.
- 1-9   92066-1466   Plug: Pressed-in type ASV hole plug. The 1996 one can be used but the new one is more convenient in view of maintenance because the new plug is pressed into the head cover. Both new and old plugs are not necessary when optional cylinderhead and magnesium head cover.
- In addition to the existing t=2.0/1.0mm ones, more variation of base gasket in different thickness to adjust squish area.
    1-12  11060-1780  Gasket  (t = 0.15mm)
    1-13  11060-1781 Gasket  (t=0.25mm)
    1-14  11060-1782 Gasket  (t=0.30mm)

### Valve-Group

- 2-1   12009-1082   Retainer-Valve Spring: New valve retainer; the form changed for more rigidity and bigger in outer diameter to increase the durability of valve spring. The 1996 one (12009-1081) can be used.
- New valve spring seat. Three-piece style from inner/outer/base elements which make the spring easier to rotate at compression for reduced mechanical loss and longer life of retainer.
  - 2-6   16007-1159   seat-spring   (base) . . . mass production part
  - 2-7   16007-1193   seat-spring   (outer)
  - 2-8   16007-1194   seat-spring   (inner)

### Camshaft

- 3-5   12048-1154   tensioner-assy: More durable cam tensioner. The 1996 one (12048-1117) can be used.
- New cam-shafts which suit both chain and gear drive system. For chain drive system, 1996 one (49118-1146 for in,-1147 for ex) can be used.
  - 3-11   49118-1156   camshaft-comp (in)
  - 3-12   49118-1157   camshaft-comp (ex)

### Piston

- 4-3   13008-1179-ring-set-piston: New piston ring set; special surface treatment to the top ring for more durability. Also reduces blow-by gas for stable performance. The 1996 one (13008-1167) can be used.

### Cover

- 8-5   11060-1783   gasket: New oil pan gasket to absorb the waving of the oil
- 8-6   55020-1616   guard: To protect left-hand side of the crankcase.

### Carburettor

9-3   99997-1084   kit-carburettor: New setting parts for FVKD41.

### Harness Gr.

- 12-3   11048-1974   bracket: New IG-coil bracket

## B. Fuel Tank and Ram-Air Case for Improving Engine Performance

### Air Filter

- New ram-air cases (upper and lower) and duct which are tighter.
  - 14-1    11011-1514   case-air filter (upper)
  - 14-2    11011-1515   case-air filter (lower)
  - 14-18   14073-1692   Duct
  - 14-19   39145-1106   Trim
- 14-17   16065-1347   carb-holder: L=23mm.

## C. Muffler Group

- 16-1   120S0825   Bolt: Length change from previous 120S0820 for exhaust header flange bolt. This is mass-production part.
- New silencer system to meet 102db regulation.
  - 16-2   18090-1600   body-comp-muffler
  - 16-3   35011-1850   stay
  - 16-9   99995-1392   kit (spare glass wool)
  - 16-7   49069-1161   muffler-assy: New exhaust system to achieve more response in low-mid range and top-end performance.

## E. Parts Group for Improving Operation Feeling

### Clutch

Needle bearing type clutch-release pusher. In accordance with this, the parts below are added:

| | | |
|---|---|---|
| 24-11 | 13114-1070 | pusher-clutch |
| 24-12 | 92046-1253 | bearing-needle |
| 24-13 | 92200-1350 | washer |
| 24-14 | 480J1500 | circlip (mass production part) |

## F. More Efficient Cooling System

- New routing. In 1996 the cooling system was designed as:
  pump→engine→oil cooler→radiator→pump
  In 1997 it is re-designed as:
  pump→engine→radiator→pump→oil cooler→pump
  Thanks to this change, as much cooler water is sent to the oil cooler, and the outlet of the cooler is directly connected to the pump, as a result more cooling capacity of engine oil is obtained. With regard to this, the following parts are added:

| | | |
|---|---|---|
| 26-33 | 39062-1713 | hose-cooling |
| 26-36 | 39062-1440 | hose-cooling (mass-production) |
| 26-34 | 92005-1330 | fitting |

- Radiator cap is separated from the upper radiator in order to avoid damage at crash. The lower radiator is also renewed.

| | | |
|---|---|---|
| 26-1 | 39060-1151 | radiator (upper) |
| 26-2 | 39060-1152 | radiator (lower) |
| 26-23 | 49044-1079 | pump-water: Chrome plating onto the shaft for more durability. |

## K. Endurance Group

### Piston Group

41-2 13001-1488   Piston engine: New piston for endurance usage. Use with endurance con-rod 13251-1115   rod-assy-connecting (46-1) and optional cylinder head (see 'L. Others'). The production piston rings (13008-1168) shall be used.

### Harness Group

42-1   26030-1502   Harness: New harness.

## L. Others

### Frame Fitting Group

- New hook-plates for rear stand;

| | | |
|---|---|---|
| 48-4 | 13270-1816 | plate (lh) |
| 48-5 | 13270-1817 | plate (rh) |
| 48-11 | 13061-1628 | boss: A boss added to apply steering damper. |

### Meter Group

50-1     25031-1049   Meter-Assy: New tachometer. The interchangability is shown in a separate table.

## Cylinder Head Group

53-1   11008-1334   head-comp-cylinder: Optional cylinder head which meets cam-gear train system. Machined combustion chamber.

### Camshaft Group

Cam-gear train system which features 3 points:
  * More durability
  * Less mechanical loss which leads more power
  * More precise recess which makes more compression ratio, which also leads to more power
3 choices of thickness for both cam/crank gear to adjust play.
Shall be applied with the optional head (53-1). When the base machine is 1996 spec, cylinder shall be replaced to 1997 production one (11005-1837).

### Crankshaft Group

* 56-1   13251-1114   rod-assy-connecting: Titanium conrod. Spare conrod bolts are supplied: 92151-1184 bolt (56-2).
* Optional bushings are available;
  |       |            |                                                                 |
  |-------|------------|-----------------------------------------------------------------|
  | 56-3  | 92028-1806 | bushing (big end) white; thinner than brown                     |
  | 56-4  | 92028-1807 | bushing (main shaft, grooved)yellow; thicker than blue          |
  | 56-5  | 92028-1808 | bushing (main shaft, grooved) white; thinner than brown         |
  | 56-6  | 92028-1809 | bushing (main shaft, w/o groove) yellow; thicker than blue      |
  | 56-7  | 92028-1810 | bushing (main shaft, w/o groove) white; thinner than brown      |

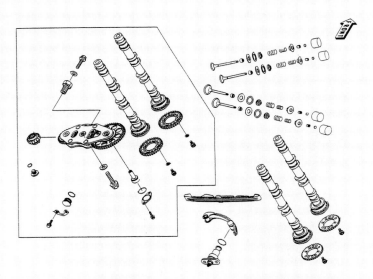

*ZX-7RR race kit showing conventional chain drive cams, and (inset) optional new-for-1997 gear-driven camshaft system.*

# 15  Retro

As the 1990s dawned, a new word was being coined for motorcycling's dictionary: *Retro*. It really started back in Japan during 1989 with a Japanese-market-only 400 Kawasaki four, named Zephyr. Then came a larger-engined model in 1990 – basically a Japanese-market 400, bored and stroked to 553cc (58 x 52.4mm). Rather than attempting to reinvent the past in contemporary form, Kawasaki had reached back into its history, and recreated a piece of it. Sold in both Japan and the USA, the 1990 ZR550-B1 Zephyr – to give the model its full title – played the nostalgia card to full effect.

Visually, the 550 Zephyr copied the hot-rodded Kawasaki streetbikes of the previous two decades, and specifically the 1000R Eddie Lawson replica – 'arguably Kawasaki's ultimate hot rod', as the American *Cycle* said in their 1990 test.

From the subtle contours of the tank and tail section to the Kerker-like, four-into-one exhaust, the 550 Zephyr looked the business; in fact Japanese aftermarket companies were soon selling lime-green bodywork to cement the connection. The irony was that the Zephyr's *American* styling was created by the Japanese themselves, and then exported back to Uncle Sam!

The engine provided a definite link to the past, being at heart the rubber-mounted, air-cooled eight-valve, across-the-frame mill based on the 1983 GPz550 – itself a tuned version of Kawasaki's 'cooking' 550 – with bigger carburettors (30 against 26mm) and lower compression ratio (9.5:1 instead of 10:1). The crankcases, cylinder and head were new castings, but the bore centres were the same, with GPz-spec crank, cams and valves; whilst the bottom end – comprising crankshaft, Hy-Vo chain primary drive and transmission ratios – was able to trace its lineage back a full decade, to Kawasaki's original KZ550 of 1980.

*In September 1990 it was announced that the Zephyr 550 'retro', which had been sold in both Japan and the USA during 1990, would thereafter be marketed on a world-wide basis.*

*A 1991 Zephyr 550 B2 (the 1990 model was coded B1). The engine was basically a bored and stroked Japanese-market 400 giving 553cc (58 x 52.4mm).*

*'Born again' biker and British touring car racer Tim Harvey with the Zephyr 550 he used to commute whilst testing on the Silverstone circuit.*

Peak power and performance levels were similar to the original 550, but despite having engine tuning similar to that of the 1982–83 GPz, the Zephyr was significantly down on power throughout the rev range compared to almost every KZ or GPz powerplant. Even Kawasaki's EN500 custom produced more peak power and torque – 50.7bhp against the Zephyr's 45.9. and 30.3lb/ft compared to 28. But that was really only half the story as the 'new' unit had a much flatter, more usable torque curve. As *Cycle* said in their test: 'Few other engines build power so linearly'. *Cycle* went on to add:

The Zephyr can also hold its own in roll-ons against the bigger, more sophisticated and more powerful sporting 600s. That's partly because, at 441.5lb (200kg), it's lighter, but more importantly it's geared significantly shorter, and isn't afflicted with the Grand Canyon torque curves of the 600s. The 550 makes at least 83 per cent of its torque available from 3,500rpm to redline. And it combines that strength with crisp throttle response, and reasonably well controlled driveline lash. So although the Kawasaki doesn't pump out dyno-rocking horse power, it puts what it has right in your hand, right where you can use it, anywhere, any time.

The torquey engine was complemented by a doublebone, double-downtube, twin shock steel chassis, with specifications and handling abilities closer to modern standards than the motor. This type of old engine/new chassis concept had already been used, most notably in the Suzuki GS500 twin, and it made good sense. Quite simply, it's easier and cheaper than developing a new engine! In fact, except for the 'add-on' of side reflectors for the Stateside market and thicker-wall rear subframe tubing, the 550 Zephyr's chassis was identical to the domestic 399cc (55 x 42mm) 400 C1 Zephyr. This had the advantage of giving a good riding position, relatively low seat height (770mm/30in) and compactness.

The 550 also inherited from the 400 a lengthy list of features that most manufacturers tend to reserve for larger, more expensive models, including dual tripmeters, lever adjusters, dual 272mm disc front brakes (with a single 217mm disc at the rear), Kawasaki's convenient eccentric chain-adjusters (carried in an aluminium swinging arm), and gas-charged integral-reservoir shocks with preload, compression and rebound damping adjustments. At the front the Zephyr was equipped with 39mm diameter stanchion telescopic forks. There were five-spoke alloy wheels, a 17in front and 18in rear tyre.

Then in September 1990 it was announced that the Zephyr 550 would be sold on a world-wide basis in 1991 as the B2 (the 1990 model was coded B1). At the same time a larger version was unveiled, the Zephyr 750C1; this was the latest Kawasaki machine developed around the philosophy of getting back to basics, to the very heart of motorcycling.

*The original 1990 specification Zephyr 550 clocks – these differ to the latest version. Note the larger tacho and basic 'no-frills' format.*

*Introduced for the 1991 season, the 750 Zephyr took the retro theme a stage further – and actually was to prove the best of the Zephyr breed.*

Clearly based on the 550, the 750 Zephyr's most notable changes were: 738cc (66 x 54mm), four 32mm Keihin CVK carbs, five-speed, 4-into-2 exhaust, 41mm forks, three-spoke wheels, 17 litres (3fl gal) fuel tank, 780mm (30.7in) seat height, 17in tyres front and rear, a 525 O-ring chain (520 on 550 model) and a dry weight of 201kg (443lb) (against 179kg (395lb)). There were six engine mounting points, two of which were rubberized to reduce engine vibration.

With its larger dual seat, grab handle for the pillion, quieter, more comprehensive exhaust and generally more sober lines, the 750 was definitely more touring than sport. But once again Kawasaki scored a bullseye, and at least for the initial period the 750 Zephyr sold well.

A year on, and in October 1991 Kawasaki took the whole retro concept a stage further, when it launched the 1100 version. Interestingly it was also at this stage that the company replaced the Zephyr tank badge with ones reading Kawasaki. This obviously signalled that Big 'K' was giving official blessing to the idea and making the series an integral part of Kawasaki's 1992 model year line-up.

Following in the footsteps of the 400, 550 and 750cc Zephyrs, the new 1100 was to be the flagship of Kawasaki's retro range; it would also play a part in other manufacturers ultimately taking a similar route. The 1,062cc (73.5 x 62.6mm) air-cooled engine was unlike its smaller brothers in that it was

*In October 1991 Kawasaki went the full hog and brought out an 1100 version of the Zephyr. The 1,062cc (73.5 x 62.6mm) was unlike its smaller brothers, in that it was largely a new unit, benefiting as it did from the company's latest big-bore four-cylinder technology.*

largely a new unit, benefiting as it did from the company's latest big-bore four-cylinder engine technology. For a start it featured a gear-driven balancer, and was specially tuned to deliver strong torque in the low and mid ranges in a way the smaller engines couldn't match, giving a relaxed riding stance and more impressive roll-on performance without the need for constant downshifting.

By using two small spark plugs per cylinder, it was possible to install 39mm intake and 34mm exhaust valves while retaining a lightweight valve-train design with inner shim-under tappet valve adjustment. The twin spark ignition provided superior propagation characteristics, with improved burn and enhanced fuel economy. The plug size was 10mm.

A pre-programmed digital ignition provided ideal ignition timing under all loads and riding conditions, while four coils delivered a strong consistent spark, with each coil supplying sparks to two plugs – one each in adjacent cylinders. For reduced exhaust emissions, the 1100 cylinder head incorporated the Kawasaki clean-air system (KCA).

Reliability was assisted by a massive seven-row oil cooler (with 50 per cent greater radiation efficiency than the 750 Zephyr), helping the engine to run at optimum operating temperatures. Twin air scoops under the tank directed a cooling air flow to special finning above the numbers two and three cylinders surrounding the spark plugs. The dohc eight-valve engine featured the largest bore ever fitted in a Kawasaki air-cooled, across-the-frame, four-cylinder engine.

There was a compression ratio of 9.1:1, four Keihin CVK 34mm carbs, five-speed gearbox, geared primary drive, and a hydraulically operated clutch incorporating a Back-Torque Limited for smoother downshifting. Chain size was up again, this time to a 530 (O-ring type).

*Out on the road, the 1100 Zephyr didn't quite perform as many hoped it would. Weighing in at a mighty 242kg (534lb) didn't help either the performance or handling, both of which left much to be desired.*

There was a high-tensile, steel, double-cradle frame with large diameter tubes, six engine mounts (the two front ones were rubberized) and a removable offside down-tube. The seat height was now 795mm (31.3in).

Dry weight had risen upwards to a decidedly lardy 242kg (533.5lb), and to help keep this extra bulk in check the fork stanchion diameter had been increased by 43mm (1.7in). Twin piggy-back reservoir nitrogen gas-charged shocks were multi-adjustable, with five-way spring preload and four-way compression and four-way rebound damping. Even so, handling and road-holding abilities were not one of the big Zephyr's best points.

The double box-section extruded aluminium swinging arm with eccentric chain adjustment was supported by two needle-roller bearings (one each side) and a single, caged ball bearing on the offside for increased strength and durability.

Braking was another area of greater size: at the front, large 310mm semi-floating discs were grabbed by four-piston calipers featuring smaller leading pistons for, claimed Kawasaki, more uniform brake pad wear and extended life. The rear brake utilized a rigidly mounted, single 240mm disc. All three discs were manufactured from stainless steel.

There were newly designed, five-spoke alloy wheels – 18in front, 17in rear. Kawasaki felt that a larger front wheel would, to quote: 'provide a stable, dignified riding characteristic'. In practice it meant a slow steering response!

When it first went on sale the 1100 Zephyr was the unquestioned King of the Retros, but unfortunately the rival Japanese manufacturers soon climbed on this particular bandwagon. First came Honda with its CB1000 Big One, next the Yamaha XJR1200, and finally in 1996 Suzuki with its 1200 Bandit. Unfortunately each one was an improvement over the other, and currently it is the much-acclaimed Bandit which wears the crown. Quite simply it has more power (100bhp) and less weight at 211kg (465lb), the result being the best performance and safest handling.

A year earlier Suzuki had also introduced its smaller Bandit, the 600, and this, too, set new standards in the middleweight retro class. Quite simply the Zephyr concept had been overtaken by the opposition – although of course there are those who are either Kawasaki stalwarts or those who just love the Zephyr in its various sizes anyway. But for the others, Kawasaki simply had to respond.

## ENTER THE ZRX1100

The answer came at the Cologne Show in September 1996, with the all-new ZRX1100 – a lean, mean and ready-for-action machine which offered potential buyers traditional muscle-bike styling with mid-1990s performance. There is no doubt that the ZRX is closer to Suzuki's Bandit than probably any other, both in performance and handling, and it certainly makes the 1100 Zephyr feel old-fashioned and heavy by comparison. It features a modified version of Kawasaki's 1990s GPZ1100 liquid-cooled, dohc sixteen-valve motor (itself based on the ZZ-R1100). Specially tuned to produce a fatter torque curve with more low-to-mid-range punch, it has ideal power characteristics for riding on both twisting back roads and faster roads with undulating, sweeping curves such as can still be found on A roads away from the motorway system.

Unlike the GPZ/ZZ-R1100 engines, that of the ZRX has the alloy cylinder block featuring cooling fins to give the engine a traditional air-cooled look. The pentroof-type combustion chambers and concave pistons run a compression ratio of 10.1:1. A new, wider-ratio, five-speed transmission capitalized on the engine's massive spread of torque for quicker acceleration from a standing start, or to provide overtaking on the open road. In the past Kawasaki has often been accused of giving its machines a less-than-perfect gear change, but on the ZRX this has been significantly improved by the use of involute splines for the transmission gears.

Outwardly resembling a 4-into-1 system, the newly designed, aluminium-plated, steel, 4-into-2-into-1 exhaust contributes to the stronger mid-range, whilst meeting all current European noise restrictions. The aluminium muffler canister provides the stylish 'race-replica' look, ample ground

*Making its public debut at the Cologne Show in September 1996, the new ZRX1100 went on sale in the UK in February 1997. With its 1990s performance and handling, plus a state-of-the-art, liquid-cooled, sixteen-valve engine, it was light years in front of the 1100 Zephyr and a serious challenger to the class-leading 1200 Suzuki Bandit.*

clearance – and it keeps the bureaucrats happy!

A quartet of Keihin CVK36 semi-flat slide, constant velocity carbs are fitted with Kawasaki's *throttle response ignition control* (K-TRIC) sensors which measure and adjust the ignition timing advance according to throttle position. This ensures optimum engine response at any engine speed or throttle opening under all types of load and riding conditions.

With its light but exceptionally strong double-cradle steel frame, state-of-the-art front suspension inherited from the ZX-6/9 line of sportsbikes, twin gas-charged piggy-back reservoir rear shocks, relatively wide handlebars and compact wheelbase (1,450mm/57in), the ZRX1100 has set out to challenge the 1200 Bandit head on.

The tubular-braced type reinforced aluminium swinging arm has a style which recreates the era of the early 1980s Superbikes. A special alumite surface treatment enhances the hi-tech, race-bred look while protecting the aluminium surface from

corrosion. Eccentric rear axle adjusters assist in helping make the chain adjustment a quick and accurate affair.

The stepped seat provides the rider with a 800mm (31.5in) low seat height which puts the rider 'in' the bike, not on it. There is a storage compartment under the lockable one-piece seat with space for an accessory U-lock (available as a optional extra). An aluminium, die-cast rear grab-rail enhances passenger comfort and security and also doubles as an additional tie-down point for carrying luggage.

Thanks to a castor angle of 25 degrees and offset of 30mm, the ZRX exhibits modern sports steering characteristics (as does the Bandit!) yet maintains composure and stability.

Tyres are another area where the ZX scores heavily over the big Zephyr: up front, a 120/70ZR17 Bridgestone BT57 radial, ably supported by a 170/60ZR17 radial at the rear.

The cartridge-type, conventional front fork features 43mm (1.7in) stanchions mated to forged aluminium bottom sliders.

*The ZRX1100 challenges Suzuki's 1200 Bandit for the honours of top retro bike.*

*The ZRX1100 features a modified version of the new GPZ1100 engine (itself based on the ZZ-R1100). Specially tuned to produce a fatter torque curve with more low- to mid-range punch, it can outrun any supercar in existence.*

*The specification includes 1,052cc (76 × 58mm) dohc, sixteen valves, liquid cooling, five speeds, six-pot calipers, braced swinging arm and bikini fairing.*

One area where the ZRX definitely matches and outshines the big Bandit is that of braking. Its twin six-piston Tokico calipers grip two, semi-floating, radially-drilled 310m stainless steel brake discs. Controlling the rear wheel is a compact, opposed-piston caliper operating on a 250mm fixed disc. A rear brake torque arm transfers rotational forces directly to the swinging arm.

However, at 222kg (489lb) the Kawasaki is a full 11kg (24.25lb) heavier than its Suzuki rival. In addition, although cheaper than its Honda and Yamaha counterparts, it's still more expensive than the Bandit by over £1,000. Only time will tell if customers will vote for the new bike with their cheque books, or continue to buy the Suzuki in such large numbers as they did in 1996. But whatever happens, the retro, like classic and vintage bikes, seems here to stay, a 1990s sales success which seems likely to transfer itself to the twenty-first century.

# Appendix

## KAWASAKI OWNER'S CLUB'S

### Kawasaki Rider's Club

The KRC is managed by Kawasaki and run by a professional team headed by Roger Burnett, former TT star and road race champion. For Social Members, the club offers a bi-monthly magazine, track days, club gatherings, ride-away trips, an annual Club Rally and even a range of Kawasaki branded clothing, as well as discount rates on road race events, travel and insurance. Full members also enjoy the benefits of a full UK breakdown and recovery service. There is a network of regional organisers providing many services for members in their local areas. Contact: Paul Farmer, KRC, Court 1, Concorde House, Kirmington Business Centre, Kirmington, South Humberside, DN39 6YP, tel. 01652 680060.

### Kawasaki GT Club

This club was established in 1988 for owners of all shaftdrive Kawasakis. They publish a monthly magazine for members to exchange news and views, report on activities, technical topics, sales and all forthcoming events. Besides local branches, there is a national rally each year. Many dealers offer discounts on spares and repairs. There are also a number of members who are experienced in foreign touring and will be more than happy to offer advice. The Kawasaki GT Club is affliliated to both the BMF and MAG. Contact: D. Shucksmith, Club Secretary, Flat K, Lichfield Court, Lichfield Road, Walsall, West Midlands, WS4 2DX.

*Bike park for Kawasaki owners at Donington Park World Superbike*

## Classic Kawasaki Club

Open to all Kawasakis over fifteen years old. Bi-monthly newsletter, insurance and other discounts. Contact: CKC, PO Box 235, Nottingham, NG8 6DT.

## Z1300 Owners Club

Formed for the benefit of Kawasaki Z1300 owners. There is a regular Wednesday evening get-together in the Cricketers Pub at Sarratt Green, Hertfordshire. The club offers techincal advice, ride outs, contacts with Z1300 clubs abroad and hold an annual rally, 'The Hillingdon Auto Show', in July. Contact: Paul Sands, tel. 01895 274230.

## Vintage Japanese Motorcycle Club

The VJMC is for owners of all older Japanese machines, not just Kawasakis, but it is still of considerable merit to owners of four- and six-cylinder Kawasakis. The Kawasaki specialist is Doug Perkins. Contact: VJMC, PO Box 515, Dartford, Kent, DA1 3RE.

## Kawasaki Z1300 Club Nederland

Dealing exclusively with the six-cylinder Z1300, the club has around 250 members, mainly in Holland but with some others in Belgium, Germany, Sweden, Denmark, South Africa and even Australia. Contact: Kawasaki Z1300 Club Nederland, Maaseikstraat 13, 1066 LX, Amsterdam, The Netherlands.

# Index

Akisade, Yasuo 158
Aldana, Dave 34
Alexandria Palace Show 83
Anderstorp Circuit 161
Assen Circuit 52
Auto Cycle Union 157
Automatic Variable
  Damping System 109,
  119, 149

Ballington, Kork 25, 131,
  162, 165
Barcelona 24-Hour Race
  161, 163
Bateman, Steve 130
Benelli 31, 39, 66, 67
Bimota, KB1 54
  KB2 40, 54
  YB4 171
Birmingham NEC Show
  124, 138
BMW 39, 91, 162
  K100 92
  K100RT 91, 96
*Bol d'Or* 52, 132, 134,
  160–2, 166
Bouton, Georges 160
Brands Hatch Circuit 36
BSA, A7 21
  A10 21
Bullock, Arthur 33

Cadwell Park Circuit 88
Campagnolo wheels 166
Carr, Cliff 34
Castle Combe Circuit 130
Chandler, Doug 132, 172
Chemarin, Jean 164–7
Charles, Prince 41
Classic Kawasaki Club 190
Cologne Show 30, 186, 187
Cornu, Jacques 164, 166,
  167
Crafer, Simon 175, 176
Crevier, Steve 134, 172
Crichton, Brian 48, 51, 127

Darley Moor Circuit 88
Daytona Circuit 34, 35, 46,
  48, 49, 171, 172
de Dion, Count 160
Dentsu Advertising Agency
  171

Denver–Chicago Endurance
  Race 160
Dixon Racing 37
Doi, Takeo 10, 11
Donington Park Circuit
  113, 171
Douaque, Pierre 163
Dowson, Michael 134, 172
Ducati 39, 87, 134, 135, 163,
  171, 172
  851 125
  916 154
du Hamel, Yvon 26, 34
Dunstall, Paul 37, 39, 40
Dürkopp 28
Dutch TT 52
Dymag wheels 166

Earls Court Show 29, 30
Eckl, Harold 175
Egli 163
Elf-Honda 163, 165
Elvington, Record Breaking
  130, 157
Emery, Dick 33
Estoril Circuit 131

Farmer, Paul 6, 189
FIM 87
Fisco Circuit 32
Flammini, Maurizio 171,
  172
FN 28, 161
Fogarty, Carl 135, 169, 173
Fontainebleau Circuit 161
Ford Sierra Car 156
Fournier, Maurice 160
Francis, Mick 88
French GP 20

Geitl, Udo 165
Gilera 31
Gobert, Anthony 135, 174–6
Godier & Genoud 163
  ZRX 1000 148
Gooding, Grant 129
Grainger, Mike 157
Grant, Mick 25, 52
Hailwood, Mike 34
Harley Davidson Electra
  Glide 66, 69
Harris 40, 55
Hickmott, Barry 111, 112

Hill, David 130
Holden, Colonel Henry 28
Honda 19, 31, 159, 162, 163,
  188
  CB 750 27–9, 162
  CB 1000 Big One 186
  CBR 600 117, 122, 123,
    125, 138, 139, 142
  CBR 1000 152
  CBR 1100R 89
  CBR 900 RR Fireblade
    116, 130, 137, 154
  CBX 69
  CX500 61, 83
  Gold Wing 66, 69
  NR 750 125
  RC 30 130, 171
  6-cylinder 66, 67
  Super Blackbird 159
  VFR 750 116
Humpstone, Dave 87
Hunt, Paul 152
Hurst, Roger 131
Isle of Man TT 52, 112, 114,
  115, 129, 130, 131
Jap-Auto Endurance Racer
  162
Jewel Sidecar 75
Johnson, Geoff 112, 114,
  115

Katatayama, Kit 52
Kawasaki
  1000 GTR 54, 91, 92, 93,
    94, 95, 96, 97, 104
  1100 Zephyr 184, 185,
    186, 187
  1100GP 48
  125 four 32
  400 Zephyr 181, 184
  550 Zephyr 182, 183, 184
  750 Turbo 42, 44, 48, 79,
    81, 82, 83, 84, 86, 87,
    88, 89, 90
  750 Zephyr 184, 185
  A1 Samurai 21, 22
  A1R 22
  A7 Avenger 22
  A7R 22
  AE50 53
  AR50 53
  B8 14, 19, 21
  EX500 Custom 183

GP 550 42, 44
GPX 1000RX 54, 91, 104,
  145, 146, 147, 148, 149,
  150, 151, 152
GPX 600 120, 121, 123,
  138
GPX 750 54, 116, 120,
  125, 126, 127, 128, 129,
  130, 131, 132, 149, 152,
  167, 168
GPZ 1100 133, 186, 188
GPz 1100 42, 44, 47, 48,
  50, 51, 82, 108, 145,
  146, 147
GPZ 250R 125, 126, 128
GPZ 500S 54, 153
GPz 550 42, 44, 48, 53,
  61, 117, 181, 183
GPz 750 48, 53, 79, 81,
  82, 90, 108, 146
GPZ 750R 42, 44, 101,
  115, 116, 117, 128, 131
GPZ600R 42, 44, 109,
  117, 118, 119, 120, 121,
  138, 148
GPZ900R 42, 44, 51, 53,
  54, 92, 102, 106,
  107–117, 127–8, 130,
  145–9
GT550 61, 62, 63, 65, 74
GT750 56, 57, 58, 59, 65,
  74
H1 22, 23, 24, 28
H1A 22
H1B 22
H1D 22
H1E 22
H1F 22
H2 22
KH 250 24
KH 400 24
KH500 22
KLR 600 54
KMX 125 54
KR250 42
KR350 42
KR500 25, 58, 165
S1 24
S2 24
S3 24
VN 1500 14, 102
VN 750 102
W1 21

W1SS 21
W2SS Commander 21
Z-1R 43, 45
Z1 6, 15, 24, 27, 28, 30, 31, 32, 33, 37, 38, 40, 52, 73, 80, 106, 130, 162
Z1000 43, 47, 52, 73, 83
Z1000 LTD 99, 100, 101
Z1000J 87, 165, 166
Z1000ST 52
Z1100 44, 53
Z1100A 51
Z1110R 50, 181
Z1300 6, 47, 52, 66, 67, 68, 69, 70, 73, 74, 75, 76, 77
Z1A 33
Z2 31, 32
Z250 Scorpion 52
Z400 42, 49
Z500 43, 49, 50, 52
Z550 42, 44, 50
Z550 LTD 52, 99, 100, 101, 103
Z650 41, 43, 44, 52, 81, 101
Z650 SR 101, 103
Z750 59
Z750 LTD 37, 52, 99, 100, 101
Z900 33, 37, 38
Z900 LTD 37, 98, 99
ZL 1000 Eliminator 102, 104
ZL 600 Eliminator 104, 105
ZL 900 Eliminator 102, 104
ZL Series 103
ZRX 1100 186, 187, 188
ZX-6R 125, 130, 138, 139, 140, 141, 142, 143, 187
ZX-7R 130, 135, 142, 143, 144, 145, 169, 172, 173, 174
ZX-7RR 143, 144, 145, 173, 175, 176, 177, 178, 179, 180
ZX-9R 130, 136, 137, 138, 139, 187
ZX10 54, 120, 122, 149, 150, 151, 152, 153, 154, 155, 156, 157
ZX11 154
ZXR 750 127, 130, 131–5, 142, 143, 167, 169, 172, 173, 174
ZXR-7 Racer 131, 132, 134
ZZ-R 600, 104, 121, 122, 123, 124, 125, 138
ZZ-R 1100 6, 14, 121, 125, 135, 136, 138, 144,

152, 153, 154, 155, 156, 157–9, 186, 188
Kawasaki GT Club 189
Kawasaki Riders' Club 189
Kawasaki, Shozo 78
Kawasaki Z1300 Club Nederland 190

Lackey, Brad 26, 42
Lambert, Michel 163
Laurin & Klement 28
Laverda 39, 162
Lawson, Eddie 49, 50, 171
Lefèvre, Gustave 161
Leguna Seca Circuit 106
Le Mans 24-Hour Race 132, 161, 167, 170
Lotus Esprit Turbo Sports Car 86
Luccinelli, Marco 171

MacPherson, Ian 176
Maguro 19, 21
Maitland Racing 45
Mang, Anton 26, 56
Manx Grand Prix 152
Matsukata, Kojiro 7
Mayhew, Stuart 87
McDiarmid, Mac 129
McLaughlin, Steve 171
Meihatsu 18
Mellor, Phil 114
Merkel, Fred 171
Mettet Circuit 163
Michaux, Ernest 160
Mihara, Shiuji 158
Milan Show 56
Milk Race 65, 95, 112
Millet, Félix Théodore 160
Moko Superbike 55
Monthléry Circuit 34, 161
Moriwaki Racing 46, 49
Morrison, Brian 134, 135, 169, 170
Mortimer Engineering 83
Moto Guzzi 39, 162
Moto Morini 87
Motosacoche 160, 161
Mower, Patrick 103
Muzzy Racing Team 132, 135, 172–6
Muzzy, Rob 173
MV Agusta 31

Nation, Trevor 114
Nielson, Cook 34
Norman, John 52
North Leicester Motorcycles 87, 88
Norton 161, 162
International 161
Nutting, John 156
Nygvist, Arto 66, 67

Österreichring Circuit 176
Owada, Shin 10
Paris–Dieppe Endurance Race 160
Paris–Prague Endurance Race 160
Patrick, Nigel 45
Paul, Rupert 130
Peckett & McNabb 161
Phase One Racing Team 169
Phillis, Rob 137, 172
Potter, Mike 119

Quattro, Suzi 102

Rainey, Wayne 171
Read Titan 37
Revill, Terry 37
Reynolds, John 122, 134, 135, 172
Rickman 37, 39, 40
Robinson, John 130
Rosset, Serge 163
Rungis Circuit 20
Russell, Scott 134, 135, 172, 173
Rymer, Terry 169, 176
Ryo, Akira 176

Santa Pod Raceway 46
Schuster, Todd 165
Seeley 40
Schmidt, Jockhim 135, 174
Schwantz, Kevin 171
Selby, Howard 129
Silverstone Circuit 168
Simmonds, Dave 6, 20, 32
Simmonds, Jennie 6, 20
Simmonds, Julie 6, 20
Singapore GP 20, 32
Slight, Arran 134, 135, 172, 173
Snetterton Circuit 24, 36, 119
Sohwa, Takahiro 134
Spa Circuit 161, 163
Spanish GP 20
Spencer, Freddie 171
Sports Marketing Company 171
Stanley Show, London 28
St. Germain Circuit 161
Strong, Peter 38
Storey, Niel 49
Sunbeam 161
Suzuka 8-Hour Race 131, 161, 173
Suzuki 19, 89
Bandit 600 186
Bandit 1200 186–8
Daytona 750 162
GS500 183

GSX-R 750 51, 125, 130, 145
GSX-R 750 W 145
XN 85 Turbo 85
RF 600 139
RF 900 153
Swann, Ray 121

Takeishi, Sinya 176
Tanaguchi, Naomi 32
Tardossi, Davide 171
Tazaki, Mr 53
Three Flags Endurance Race 160
Thruxton Circuit 161
Tokyo Show 28, 80
Triumph Speed Twin 28
1200 Daytona 125
Tukuno, Masaki 46, 48
Turner, Edward 28

Uchida, Mick 38, 52
Uni-Trak rear suspension 42, 50, 96, 119, 131, 132, 139, 148, 152, 165, 167, 171, 173

Vaujours Circuit 160
Vauxhall Cavalier SRi Car 156
Velocette 87, 161
Vincent 87
Vincent, Chris 32
Vink, Henk 46
Vintage Japanese Motorcycle Club 190
Vogt, Dipl. Ing. Richard 11

Wada, Masahiro 34
Warnell ZI Superbike 40
Wells, Jim 161
Werner, Eugene 160
Werner, Michel 160
Wilson, Ian 113
Wilvert, Hurley 34
Woodhall, Adam 119

Yamaha 19, 39, 188
DT 125 54
FJ 1200 102, 153, 157
FZ 750 51
FZR 600 122, 123, 139
FZR 1000 152
OW01 171
TZ 350 162
V-Max 102
XJR 1200 186
XS 750 162
Yanagawa, Akira 176
Yoshimura, Pops Jnr. 162

Zolder Circuit 161
Z1300 Owners' Club 190